THE
DEE BRESTIN
BIBLE STUDY SERIES

A WOMAN
OF
Hospitality

The Dee Brestin Series
From Cook Communications

BOOKS

The Friendships of Women
The Friendships of Women Devotional Journal

We Are Sisters
We Are Sisters Devotional Journal

BIBLE STUDY GUIDES

A WOMAN OF LOVE
Using Our Gift for Intimacy (Ruth)

A WOMAN OF FAITH
Overcoming the World's Influences (Esther)

A WOMAN OF CONFIDENCE
Triumphing over Life's Trials (1 Peter)

A WOMAN OF PURPOSE
Walking with the Savior (Luke)

A WOMAN OF WORSHIP
Praying with Power (10 psalms with a music CD)

A WOMAN OF HOSPITALITY
Loving the Biblical Approach (Topical)

A WOMAN OF MODERATION
Breaking the Chains of Poor Eating Habits (Topical)

A WOMAN OF CONTENTMENT
Insight into Life's Sorrows (Ecclesiastes)

A WOMAN OF BEAUTY
Becoming More Like Jesus (1, 2, 3 John)

A WOMAN OF WISDOM
God's Practical Advice for Living (Proverbs)

A WOMAN OF HEALTHY RELATIONSHIPS
Sisters, Mothers, Daughters, Friends (Topical)

THE FRIENDSHIPS OF WOMEN BIBLE STUDY GUIDE correlates with THE FRIENDSHIPS OF WOMEN

NexGen® is an imprint of
Cook Communications Ministries, Colorado Springs, CO 80918
Cook Communications, Paris, Ontario
Kingsway Communications, Eastbourne, England

A WOMAN OF HOSPITALITY
© 2006 by Dee Brestin

First printing, 2005
Printed in Canada

1 2 3 4 5 6 7 8 9 10 Printing/Year 10 09 08 07 06 05

Cover Design: Greg Jackson, Thinkpen Design, llc
Interior Design: Nancy L. Haskins

Unless otherwise noted, Scripture quotations are taken from the HOLY BIBLE, NEW INTERNATIONAL VERSION®. Copyright © 1973, 1978, 1984 International Bible Society. Used by permission of Zondervan Publishing House. All rights reserved. Scripture quotations marked MSG are taken from THE MESSAGE. Copyright © 1993, 1994, 1995, 1996, 2000, 2001, 2002 by Eugene H. Peterson. Used by permission of NavPress Publishing Group. All rights reserved. Scripture quotations marked PH are taken from J.B. Phillips: The New Testament in Modern English, revised editions © J.B. Phillips, 1958, 1960, 1972, permission of Macmillan Publishing Co. and Collins Publishers. Scripture quotations marked KJV are taken from the King James Version of the Bible. Scripture quotations marked NKJV are taken from the New King James Version®. Copyright © 1982 by Thomas Nelson, Inc. Used by permission. All rights reserved. Scripture quotations marked NLT are taken from the Holy Bible, New Living Translation, Copyright © 1996. Used by permission of Tyndale House Publishers, Inc., Wheaton, Illinois, 60189. All rights reserved.

ISBN: 0-78144-333-4

Contents

To my daughter-in-law Julie,

Whose Hospitality Changes Lives

Introduction

As babes in Christ, my husband and I were strengthened tremendously by mature Christians who practiced hospitality. We moved many times in those early years, but believers reached out to us and invited us into their homes. As we broke bread with them at candlelit tables, the conversations often flowed to spiritual things. As we were ministered to, in those formative years, we learned to minister.

It then became our practice to invite people to our home for tea, meals, overnight visits, and sometimes to live with us for a time. We have seen God heal broken hearts and souls, we have been blessed by rich friendships, and we have seen our children transformed by ministering and being ministered to by guests.

Now that some of our children are grown, we see *them* practicing biblical hospitality, inviting "strangers" over, and inviting those in need to stay with them temporarily.

When our son and daughter-in-law were riding a bus in their city of Lincoln, Nebraska, they struck up a conversation with a young Hispanic woman. They discovered Nancy had been in America only a week and was missing her parents and siblings in Argentina. Spontaneously, they invited her home for supper, and the following weekend she came with them to join us for a family ski trip to Colorado. How we loved this charming young woman!

We were so glad when she visited us again at Easter. I hid small Easter baskets for everyone on our roof, with the clue, "Jesus ROSE from the dead and ASCENDED into heaven." When they finally found the baskets, Nancy, with eyes shining, said: "What a wonderful American custom—this hiding of candy baskets on the roof!" We laughed.

A few days later Nancy wrote me a letter which brought tears to my eyes:

> I am so far away from my family, and I miss them so. I am real-
> izing how much I love and appreciate them. And yet in those
> times when loneliness wells up in me, it is made easier by you
> and your family, who take me into your home, and give me
> fondness. You are my family here, and for that my heart is full
> of gratitude.

A Christian home is a miracle to be shared. If believers would understand
God's model and practice it, I am convinced they would love it, for the
promise of God in 1 John is that as we love others, our love is made complete (1 John 4:12). This study is addressed to women, for women are usually the soul of the home. Whether hospitality is being shown to the family, extended family, or to those in spiritual, emotional, or physical need—
the woman is usually key.

Some of us aren't hospitable because our homes are so messy. Marla
Cilley, also known as "The Fly Lady" (flylady.net) asks if you are afflicted
with CHAOS (Can't Have Anyone Over Syndrome)? If you dread the
thought of anyone walking through your door because you live in an
absolutes chaos, then you need to ask a Christian sister for help! Look for
a mentor—a friend who has victory in this area, and humbly ask for help.
Often one afternoon with mentoring help can get you started on the road
to success. Or, it may be that your problem is that you have confused
entertaining with hospitality, in which case the first less will put your
heart at rest.

You can either do the first chapter ahead of time or together with your
small group. However, beginning with Chapter 2, group members need to
work ahead of time. You will find daily assignments to encourage the
habit of meeting daily with the Lord and Action Assignments to encourage the habit of applying God's Word.

Leader's Helps are at the back as well as blank pages for prayers and
praises.

One

How Does Hospitality Differ from Entertaining?

*O*pen Heart, Open Home (InterVarsity Press, 1976) by Karen Mains is a classic title on hospitality. Mains says: "Entertaining has little to do with real hospitality." This chapter will help you discover why.

WARMUP

Make a name tag for yourself with the supplies your discussion leader has brought. Make a shape or a drawing that symbolizes something about yourself. Some examples:

> *A violet: "I tend to be a shrinking violet in new groups—it takes me a little while to feel at ease."*

> *A car full of children: "I live in the country and spend a good part of my day chauffeuring my three children."*

> *An uprooted tree: "I just moved here and am eager to put down roots."*

Share what your name tag means, and why you've come to this group.

If your group is new, go around again. Share your name, and everyone's first name who has spoken (i.e., "My name is Dee, and this is Beth, and Sharon, and Nancy").

The essence of hospitality is to, through service, be *a vehicle through which God's grace can flow* (1 Peter 4:9–10). Consider how the following efforts would demonstrate a hospitable spirit to the other women in your small group:

    A. Making these meetings a priority

    B. Doing your homework ahead of time

    C. Sharing if you are naturally shy; holding back if you are naturally talkative

SCRIPTURE STUDY

A Model of Entertaining

Read Esther 1:1–9 aloud.

Notice that this banquet was given shortly before Xerxes persuaded other Persian military leaders to invade Greece.

1. Who was invited to this banquet? (v. 3) What was Xerxes' motive in hosting this party? (v. 4)

2. List some ways Xerxes impressed his guests (vv. 4–8).

In *The Gracious Woman* (Harvest House, 1985), author June Curtis remembers the advice the Dean of the Law School gave the wives when their husbands graduated: "To be an asset to your husband's practice, join every organization you can. Entertain as much as possible. It's important to make friends with the right people."

3. List some possible worldly purposes of entertaining. Who is likely to be invited to your home—and why? What are some ways people endeavor to impress their guests?

Karen Mains writes: "Entertaining says, 'I want to impress you with my beautiful home, my clever decorating, my gourmet cooking.' . . . Entertaining looks for payment. . . . Hospitality, however, seeks to minister. It says, 'This home is not mine. It is truly a gift from my Master. I am His servant and I use it as He desires.' Hospitality does not try to impress, but to serve."

Read Esther 1:10–22.

The Targum, an ancient paraphrase of the Old Testament, indicates that Queen Vashti was ordered to appear naked, except for her crown. Josephus, a Jewish historian, says this is probable. Whether or not this is true, it is clear that Xerxes' command was demeaning. It was like asking Vashti to pop out of a cardboard cake. In entertaining, the focus is on the host's wants. But in hospitality, it is completely reversed: The guest is the focus.

4. What was Xerxes' motive in inviting Vashti to his party? (v. 11) How did it backfire?

5. If Xerxes' motive in inviting Vashti to his banquet had been to honor or serve her in love, how might he have treated her differently?

6. How did Xerxes and his counselors plan revenge on Vashti?

My pastor friend, John Bronson, sums up Esther 1:15–21 this way: "Women, heel! If you don't, we will crush you!" Xerxes was trying to recover the ground he lost with his guests resulting from Vashti's embarrassing refusal.

7. Why does entertaining make you more vulnerable to embarrassment than hospitality? Can you share a time when, in desiring to make an impression, you flopped and were embarrassed? Or a time when guests dropped by unexpectedly and all you could think about was your messy house?

A MODEL OF HOSPITALITY

Read 2 Kings 4:8–17.

8. Whom did the Shunammite woman want to feel welcome in her home? How did she do this? (v. 10)

9. What do you think her motive was? (v. 9)

10. How was the Shunammite woman blessed for her hospitality? (vv. 11–17) Do you think she was hospitable in order to gain something? Why or why not?

11. Give a specific example of how you have been blessed for showing hospitality.

Read Luke 14:12–14.

12. Whom does Jesus tell us to invite into our home for meals? Why?

Read Luke 10:38–42.

This is a marvelous story. Here we see what Jesus valued. It is amazing that He protected Mary. The general view of women was that they were second-class citizens, not allowed to sit at the feet of a rabbi. They belonged in the kitchen! Yet here, as He so often does, Jesus reverses this. He also clearly says that what Mary has chosen is better. She has chosen to sit at His feet, drink in His words, and love Him with all her heart, soul, and mind. Some may object, saying Martha was showing love as well. But remember, Jesus could see her heart. He knew her focus was on herself.

13. Look at the pronouns in verse 38. How many men came?

Although we often picture thirteen men in this scene, the pronouns indicate Jesus was alone.

14. How is Mary described in this scene? How is Martha described?

15. What does Jesus say to Martha?

Jesus would have preferred she sit down, like her sister Mary, and listen. On the radio program, "Insight for Living," Charles Swindoll put it like this: "Martha, Martha—chips and dips would be great." Swindoll says Jesus came for the fellowship rather than the food.

16. What is the central point of this story?

So often we, as women, can feel hurt by this story. Jesus was not rebuking Martha for her service, but for her attitude, and for being so busy about many things that she missed the most important thing—listening to Jesus, loving Jesus, seizing this rare moment to be with Him. It is absolutely wonderful that Jesus protected Mary and cared enough about Martha to gently rebuke her.

17. Be still before the Lord. If He were to talk to you about your ways of hospitality, what do you think He would say?

18. What does Proverbs 20:5 teach?

When my husband was looking for a medical practice, I remember being invited spontaneously to a potential partner's home for lunch. The partner's wife, Margie, had no warning but eagerly welcomed me, opened a can of soup and a can of peaches, and peppered me with questions, making me feel special and interesting. She helped me, through her questions, consider what my husband and I were really looking for in a practice. She drew out the deep waters of my soul. And she never apologized for her simple lunch or her slightly messy house. Her focus was definitely on me rather than herself—and she made me feel like a queen.

19. Compare the differences or similarities in entertaining and hospitality.

	Entertaining	Hospitality
Motives		
Guest List		
Focus		
Rewards		

20. What are some ways people have made you feel cared for and wanted in their homes? Give specific examples of what it was they did or said that made you feel loved.

21. How might you do this for anyone who comes into your home (family, friend, neighborhood child) this week?

22. What do you think you'll remember from today's Scriptures and discussion that you could apply to your life? (If time permits, hear from everyone, giving women the freedom to pass.)

Women have told me that they were helped by my showing them how to memorize Scripture by doing a word at a time. Together, memorize Proverbs 20:5 (*The purposes of a man's heart are deep waters, but a man of understanding draws them out*) by saying:

Proverbs

Proverbs 20

Proverbs 20:5

Proverbs 20:5 "The

Proverbs 20:5 "The purposes

Proverbs 20:5 "The purposes of

Proverbs 20:5 "The purposes of a ...

Review it every day, and you'll know the verse in a week! Whether you serve soup or roast lamb, your guests will be ministered to if you have mastered the art of drawing out the deep waters of their hearts. Learning which questions to ask is an important ingredient of hospitality. Next week we will be looking at the ingredients of hospitality. As you practice your verse, apply it with the people in your life!

PRAYER TIME

Many people are intimidated by the idea of praying out loud. This guide will be gentle, leading you into this slowly. And no one will ever be forced to pray out loud.

Today, everyone may pray the following prayer in unison:

Father, help me to understand what it really means to be hospitable. Show me how I can use this art to honor You. Make me aware of the people in my life to whom You would like me to be hospitable.

Be sure to get started on your daily assignment in Chapter 2 tomorrow!

Also, at the end of every chapter, you will find a Prayers and Praises page. Use this space to write out your petitions and thanks to the Lord as you learn more about hospitality and apply it to your life. You will enjoy looking back over your journey when you complete this guide!

Prayers & Praises

Two
A Heart for Hospitality

The practice of hospitality is modeled throughout the pages of the Old and New Testaments. We are exhorted to "Offer hospitality to one another without grumbling" (1 Peter 4:9). Again and again, Scripture shows that the purpose of the host or hostess was to serve others, to be a vehicle for God's grace (1 Peter 4:10). The first, and essential ingredient is the love of Christ shed abroad in our hearts. Unless we have His love overflowing in our hearts, we will be practicing entertaining instead of hospitality. A heart filled with His love will be a vehicle for His grace. Other ingredients may vary, but frequently in Scripture we see: a warm welcome, the breaking of bread, a special sensitivity to the words and needs of the guest, and a fond farewell. In this chapter, we will look at two model hosts from the Old Testament: Abraham and Boaz.

WARMUP

Pair off and spend a few minutes drawing out your partner in conversation to get to know her better. Then go around the room and have each person introduce her partner to the group. For example:

This is Jean. She's been adjusting to an empty nest and misses nurturing her children, as she's a natural nurturer! She's still busy nurturing her husband, her kindergarten students, and girls who come to the Crisis Pregnancy Clinic where she serves as a volunteer.

Share your memory verse (see Day 1, page 19) and any thoughts about it.

SCRIPTURE STUDY

DAY 1

. . . .

A Heart Transplant

We are naturally selfish, putting our own needs before the needs of others. We naturally have ulterior motives for having others into our homes. We naturally want to talk about ourselves rather than drawing out the deep waters of another's soul. We need a heart transplant! Then, on a daily basis, we need to live in repentance for how easily we return to our old ways. The flesh struggles against us, but God longs to give us victory in Christ. Of all the ingredients of hospitality, this is the essential one. If you have a new heart and if you are walking in daily repentance, then the love of God will flow through you. You'll not only be aware, but truly caring of the people in your path, making you eager to bless them and put their needs above your own. This is what Jesus did, and this is the essence of true hospitality.

Read Romans 5:6–11.

1. A. Write down everything you can discover about Christ's death for us from verses 6–8.

   B. What changes occur in one who has trusted in Christ's blood for his salvation? (vv. 9–11)

2. Read Ephesians 4:22—5:21. What, according to the following verses, should characterize those who have had a heart transplant? In each case, imagine how this would be lived out in the practice of hospitality.

Ephesians 4:25

Ephesians 4:29

Some of the greatest growth in my life has occurred because caring brothers or sisters were willing to speak the truth in love to me. I knew they really loved me because they had demonstrated that love in many ways, and when their conversation was seasoned with grace, I could hear them about an area where I was weak. I listened when a godly woman told me I needed to follow through when I set boundaries for my little boy; I listened when my sister encouraged me to read meatier books; and I responded when my friend told me she sensed a lack of love in me toward a particular person. Too often in the body of Christ we let offenses grow, or we speak "sideways," and the person doesn't get it, or we lose our temper and speak in anger. A book that has helped me enormously in having that difficult conversation is *Boundaries Face to Face: How to Have That Difficult Conversation You've Been Avoiding* by Dr. Henry Cloud and Dr. John Townsend.

Ephesians 4:32

Ephesians 5:1-2

Ephesians 5:15-16

Ephesians 5:19-20

I cannot do any of the above myself. I must continually cry out for mercy, asking the Lord to live through me.

Memory Verse

Begin memorizing Proverbs 20:5. Review this each day, meditate on it, and practice drawing out the deep waters of your friends and family!

> *The purposes of a man's heart are deep waters, but a man of understanding draws them out* (Prov. 20:5).

Action Assignment #1

Sometime this week, draw out the deep waters of another's soul by asking the following questions of someone to whom you are close. (You can either ask all the questions to one person or divide them between people.) Record their answers to enhance your listening skills.

What have you been thinking about today and yesterday? Has your mind been going back to a problem, a person, a need?

Tell me about a time, either recently or in the past, when you were acutely aware of God working in your life.

Tell me about something that you are thankful for which you couldn't have been thankful for last year.

DAY 2

A Heart like His

Not only do we need a heart transplant, but then we need to care for that new heart, keeping it clean by living in daily repentance. John's letters, addressed to believers, challenge us to walk in that repentance. While these letters are covered in depth in another guide, we will look today at the basic truths John teaches in them. He continually stressed that if we are born of God, then we will be like Him. When someone interacts with us—whether it is in our home over a meal or at work at the coffee pot—if our hearts are right, than that person experiences something of Jesus. In *Mere Christianity*, C. S. Lewis puts it like this:

> Good things, as well as bad, you know, are caught by infection. If you want to be warm, you must stand near the fire; if you want to get wet, you must get into the water. If you want joy, power, peace, eternal life, you must get close to, or even into, the thing that has them. . . . [Christ] came to this world and became a man in order to spread to other men the kind of life He has—by what I call "good infection." Every Christian is to become a little Christ.

> (C. S. Lewis, *Mere Christianity*, p. 153)

John's gospel tells us that as we abide in Him, we *will* bear fruit—fruit that will last. The fruit of the Spirit is love, joy, peace, gentleness—the characteristics of the hospitable Christ.

John's letter tells us the same. God is light, God is love, God is truth, and God is mercy—therefore, if we have the life of God living in us, we will be light, love, truth, and mercy. Every time we are aware that is not true of us, we must repent, U-turn, trust Christ's blood to make us clean again, run to Him, and abide in Him daily.

Another wonderfully exciting truth John teaches is that as we obey and love, Christ's love becomes *complete* in us. I have often noticed that truly hospitable Christians seem to be *especially loving*. Could it be they were not always so? Could it be that practicing Christian hospitality has made God's love complete in them? I believe it to be, for that is what the Word teaches.

3. According to 1 John 1:1-4, describe what John is proclaiming (v. 2) and why (v. 3).

The goal of true hospitality is to allow others to experience the love of Christ. Christian hospitality is deeper than any other kind of fellowship—for it involves Jesus, who lives in us.

4. In the following passages, write down first what you learn about God, and then how we can be like Him.

1 John 1:5 and 1:9

1 John 3:16–18

5. What is taught about becoming complete in the following passages?

1 John 2:5

1 John 4:12

6. What have you learned today that could be relevant to hospitality?

DAY 3

A Warm Welcome and a Warm Farewell

Today you will look first at Jesus, who welcomed all kinds of people into His life. And though Jesus did not have a home, He was hospitable, for hospitality has to do with the heart. In the Greek, hospitality means "fond of guests." Jesus was fond of all kinds of "guests." Jesus was often interrupted by people with needs; and He consistently responded with a warm welcome, sensitivity to the need, and often, an important word as they left.

Then we will look at two men from the Old Testament who model hospitality. Each of these men trusted God, and His life was vibrant in them. This is apparent from the moment their paths crossed with the path of a stranger. How warmly the stranger was welcomed! What a wonderful model for us as our paths interact with people throughout the day.

Review your memory verse, meditate on it, and apply it!

7. Describe who Jesus welcomed and how He communicated that welcome in each of the following incidents from Luke's gospel.

Luke 5:18–20

Luke 5:29–31

Jesus seeks out those in need who sense their position before God. The Pharisees, as the "healthy," are not prepared to be treated for something they do not recognize as diseased (Dr. Darrell Bock, *Luke*, Volume I, p. 498).

Luke 7:11–15

Luke 7:36–50

Luke 19:1–10

8. In a sentence, summarize how Jesus exhibited a welcoming spirit to others.

Read Genesis 18:1–5.
9. A. How did Abraham make it clear that he was sincere about wanting the men to stop and be refreshed? List everything you can find.

B. Why do you think Abraham was so eager?

C. How can you discern a sincere invitation from an insincere one?

D. Whom do you think Abraham's guests were? (See Genesis 19:1 and Hebrews 13:2.) Angels may be in disguise, sent by God to deliver a personal message. Is it possible that you've been visited by an angel? If so, share something about it.

These three guests were the Lord and two angels (The Bible Knowledge Commentary, Victor, 1985).

Read Ruth 2:1–12.

10. A. How did Boaz greet the harvesters? How did they greet him? (v. 4)

B. The harvesters' prayer was answered quickly. How? (v. 5)

C. What are some better ways to greet people than: "How are you?"

D. How did Boaz greet Ruth? (vv. 8–9) How did she respond? (v. 10) And then how did he reassure her? (vv. 11–12)

E. How do you think Boaz's greeting to Ruth dispersed her fears and made her feel welcome? How might you do the same with your guests?

Missionary Sara Regier tells of learning the custom of "giving greetings" from the people of Zaire in Doris Longacre's book, *Living More With Less* (Herald Press, 1980). The first thing they do when guests arrive is to welcome them and *sit down* with them. "First the guest tells about himself without interruption: his trip, what has happened since we last saw each other, the purpose of the visit. Then the host gives a response. This exchange is a good listening exercise and important for communication. . . . Sharing these first moments is important in sensing their mood. . . . We get clues as to their needs."

11. What are some ways people have made you feel warmly welcomed by the way they invited you or greeted you? Do you sit down with guests initially or are you consumed by food preparation?

12. If you live with a family or roommate, how do you greet them when they come home? How do you like to be greeted?

13. If you work outside of the home, how do you greet people each morning at work? Do you think they can sense the love of Christ in your greeting?

Just as a warm welcome is important, so is a warm farewell. Whether you are saying good-bye for the day or for, perhaps, a lifetime, important things are said in closing moments. Jesus said His most important things when time was running out. But even small partings are important. A friend can sense whether you are glad he's going or whether you care enough to make this farewell meaningful.

Read Genesis 18:16.

14. Describe how Abraham made his guests feel cared for in parting from them.

Read 1 Samuel 20:41–42.

15. What do you learn from this scene about saying good-bye to someone you love who is going to be gone for a long period of time?

> The most meaningful moments of a friend's visit may occur when I take the trouble to walk her to her car. The very act of showing that I care enough to prolong the visit often releases from her a confidence or expression of love that we both treasure. The more final the good-bye, the greater the bleeding, but the more cherished the memory.... Closing expressions of love may give consolation for years to come. If I'm not willing to create these parting scenes, then they slip between the cracks of time, never to be called to remembrance when remembrance is sorely needed (Dee Brestin, *The Friendships of Women*, Victor, 1988).

16. Brainstorm some fresh ways to see loved ones on their way (friends, children, spouses) to make them feel loved, appreciated, and more prepared to face whatever they are facing.

My daughter-in-law prays for her four children each morning before they walk out the door for school. Circling them in her arms, she prays that God will keep their hearts and minds safe in Christ Jesus and that they will each be a light of Jesus' love.

DAY 4

Breaking Bread Together

Breaking bread is not essential to hospitality. However, Scripture models the breaking of bread, for it seems we are more open to one another over a meal. In today's hurried world, many families have stopped eating together. At one time, inviting church visitors home to Sunday dinner was common practice but now it's a rarity. Yet our Lord often chose to communicate important truths over the breaking of bread, and the Scripture is full of examples of saints who did likewise. We will look first at Jesus and then return to our Old Testament examples of Abraham and Boaz.

17. In the following accounts, what happened in *addition* to the breaking of bread?

Matthew 26:26–29

Luke 24:30–35

John 21

18. Why do you think that important communication often happens over a meal?

Latayne C. Scott, in *Open Up Your Life* (Zondervan, 1983), comments that breaking bread together helps us to see one another as family. Families eat together and food also reminds us of our dependence on God's provision. Jesus ate with His friends at His first miracle (the wedding at Cana) and at His last miracle (the disciples' miraculous catch of fish).

Read Genesis 18:6–8.

19. A. Describe what was involved in preparing a meal for these guests.

    B. How did Abraham's preparations show the guests he was honoring them?

    C. Share a time when you were honored by elaborate food preparations.

Read Ruth 2:14–16.

20. A. Describe everything Boaz did for Ruth. Remembering that Ruth was a foreigner, a Moabite, how might this have ministered to her?

    B. Contrast Abraham's preparations with those of Boaz.

    C. Share a time when you were honored by simple food preparations.

Read the following two differing opinions:

> On our last visit to Canada and the United States we were surprised and even shocked to note how often people eat out. Instead of cooking a meal and having people "in," the trend was to entertain at a restaurant. We remember looking forward to spending an evening in the home of friends. When we arrived, we all piled into their car and drove across town to eat out. We all knew the hostess was a super cook, so this added to our disappointment (John and Tina Bohn, from Doris Longacre's *Living More With Less,* Herald Press, 1980).

> Don't feel you must provide a meal or entertainment to invite people into your home for fellowship. There is absolutely nothing wrong with inviting friends over after supper, for a glass of iced tea, or to enjoy take-out food.... If you are too exhausted to think about

food, stop by a delicatessen or take your guests out to eat (Rachael Crabb, *The Personal Touch: Encouraging Others Through Hospitality*, NavPress, 1990).

21. Ecclesiastes 3:1 tells us: *"There is a time for everything and a season for every activity under heaven."* When is it time to be elaborate? To be simple? What truths do you find in each of the above opinions?

22. What is it about breaking bread with another that binds you together? Have you experienced this? Comment.

DAY 5

Sensitivity to the Needs of Others

Whether He was a guest or a host, the focus of Jesus was always on the person, never on Himself. He discerned what each person needed and set about meeting that need. As Christ lives in us, we must allow that same sensitivity, love, and grace to flow through us.

Read Philippians 2:1–11.

23. A. What are some of the good gifts a person who truly knows Jesus should be experiencing? (v. 1)

B. What will make Paul's joy complete? (v. 2)

C. What should be our goal? (vv. 3-4)

D. Who is our example and how did He powerfully set that example? (vv. 5-8)

Examine Ruth 2:1–23.

24. Find all the ways Boaz was sensitive to Ruth's needs that you haven't mentioned before.

25. How might you apply Proverbs 20:5 to a guest? What makes a good listener?

> I always try to steer those I talk with
> back to the subjects they know best.
> *(Essays of Montaigne,* Book I, Essay 17)

26. Imagine a guest has just made one of the following statements to you. How might you respond to him in a way that would draw him out and minister to him? Also, what kind of responses would do the opposite?

    A. "I just saw the movie *Chariots of Fire* (or another movie) and really enjoyed it."

    B. "School has really been frustrating to me lately."

27. List some of the ingredients of hospitality you've studied this week. What stands out to you and why?

Action Assignment

What did you do? What did you learn?

PRAYER TIME

Today, take time for prayer requests and write them down on the next page.

At least once this week, pray through this list.

If your group is large, divide into smaller groups of five or six.

Stand in a circle, holding hands. Each woman should say a sentence prayer for the prayer request of the woman on her right. That prayer can be as simple as, "Lord, bless Nancy." If she feels she cannot say that, she should squeeze Nancy's hand and that will be a signal to Nancy to pray for the woman on her right.

Prayers & Praises

_____

_____

_____

_____

_____

_____

_____

_____

_____

_____

_____

_____

_____

_____

Three
The Dance of Hospitality

When I first fell in love with Jesus, oh, how we danced! Like Anna in *The King and I*—I was flying across the dance floor with the most Magnificent Dancer. I heard the music, abandoned myself to His lead, and danced like I never could have danced alone.

But as time passes, it's easy to take Jesus for granted, to stop listening for the music, and to resist the gentle pressure from His hand in the small of your back.

I wanted to sit the dance out when our pastor suggested that a young couple from Nepal move in with us. "Hari is a new Christian—but his nineteen-year-old bride doesn't know the Lord and is terribly homesick. Could you find it in your heart to have them move in for a few months?"

I promised to pray. And when I prayed, God did a work in my heart. I let Him take my hand and lead me back to the dance floor.

The day Hari and Rita moved in, tiny Rita hid behind Hari, giggling. She peeked out and her dark eyes lit up when she saw me. "Auntie?" How I remember when Hari asked our teenage daughter to make Rita's legs smooth, like the legs of American ladies. Rita and Sally disappeared into the bathroom and we heard water splashing, Rita shrieking, and Sally laughing. When they emerged, Rita was beaming. She put her leg proudly up on the chair and insisted we all run our hands over her smooth skin. Rita was so easy to love.

Since Rita's English was limited, we acted out Bible stories and used big children's picture books to tell her about Jesus. She loved the stories, but when her English improved, she said, "Jesus American god. I worship Jesus now—but when we go home to Nepal, I worship Buddha."

Their first baby came along and they moved into their own apartment. Then Rita became pregnant again, but this time the pregnancy was mysteriously difficult. How shocked I was when the doctor called to tell me that Rita, at twenty-three, had terminal cancer. Suddenly the dance became a slow and somber one.

The last time I saw Rita she lay weakly on the sofa holding her newborn baby. When I walked into the room, her face brightened: "Auntie! I tell you something! I know Jesus!"

"Oh, Rita," I said, my tears flowing. "How wonderful!"

"I see Jesus soon, Auntie. So I need favor."

I thought, *Oh no—she's going to give me her children.*

Instead, she said, "I need you to find a good wife for Hari, a good mother for Angela and Andrew. She must love Jesus. Okay, Auntie?"

"Okay Rita," I promised. *Help me, Lord.*

A few months after Rita's death, Hari called: "Do you have a wife for me?"

"I need a little time, Hari!"

"Call me as soon as you find her!"

Christy was a radiant young woman in my Bible study. The day I sensed the Lord leading me toward her was the day Christy told me: "Guess how I'm spending my break!"

"Skiing? A mission trip?"

"I'm babysitting for my best friend's children while they go on vacation. I can't wait!"

I think you may be the one. I called Hari and told him about Christy. He said: "Dee, set me up for ten dates!"

I laughed. "In America, you get *one,* Hari. Then we'll see what the Lord does."

The Lord did amazing things. Today Hari and Christy are raising their three children (Alicia came along two years after their wedding) to love Jesus and mentoring college students to hear the music and participate in the dance.

I'm so glad I didn't sit this dance out. He has gifted women to be relational, to make a difference in the lives of others. But we must listen to the music, let Him lead us onto the dance floor, and stay close to His heart. And oh, how we'll dance!

(The above story first appeared in *American Missionary Fellowship*— Fall/2004)

This week we will study Rahab, and how she took the Lord's hand and entered the dance, saving the lives of many. The story of Rahab beautifully demonstrates the link between hospitality and faith. Though we will probably not be asked to risk our lives, as Rahab did, we will definitely face risks of a lesser degree in seeking to minister to those in need. I have discovered that those who shield themselves from risks miss so much. They miss the dance, the deep friendships that risk-takers have, and the joy of seeing God's love being made complete in them.

WARMUP

Act out Rahab's story from Joshua 2 using the following script. If you don't have enough people for the supporting characters, you can imagine them. (Don't be shy and sit the dance out. You'll have fun, and the story will come to life in a way that it couldn't through reading it.)

PROPS:

- blanket
- scarlet cord
- thread

CAST:

- Narrator
- Rahab
- 2 Israelite spies
- Jericho police

SCENE I

Narrator: Rahab was home when the Israelite spies knocked on her door. (SPIES KNOCK ON DOOR.) When Rahab discovered the Israelites at the door, she took them up to the roof and had them lie down under the stalks of flax. (RAHAB PRETENDS TO CLIMB STAIRS AND PUTS BLANKET OVER SPIES.)

SCENE 2

Narrator: The king of Jericho was told: "Look! Some of the Israelites have come here tonight to spy out the land." So the king of Jericho sent his police with this message to Rahab.

Police: (JERICHO POLICE KNOCK ON RAHAB'S DOOR. RAHAB OPENS IT.) Bring out the men who came to you and entered your house, because they have come to spy out the whole land.

Rahab: Yes, the men came to me, but I did not know where they had come from. At dusk, when it was time to close the city gate, the men left. I don't know which way they went. Go after them quickly. You may catch up with them. (POLICE RUN OUT OF THE ROOM.)

Narrator: So the police set out in pursuit of the spies on the road that leads to the fords of the Jordan, and as soon as the pursuers had gone out, the gate was shut. Rahab then went up on the roof and spoke to the spies.

Rahab: I know that the Lord has given this land to you and that a great fear of you has fallen on us, so that all who live in this country are melting in fear because of you. We have heard how the Lord dried up the water of the Red Sea for you when you came out of Egypt, and what you did to Sihon and Og, the two kings of the Amorites east of the Jordan, whom you completely destroyed. When we heard of it, our hearts melted and everyone's courage failed because of you, for the Lord your God is God in heaven above and on the earth below. Now then, please swear to me by the Lord that you will show kindness to my family, because I have shown kindness to you. Give me a sure sign that you will spare the lives of my father and mother, my brothers and sisters, and all who belong to them, and that you will save us from death.

Spies: Our lives for your lives! If you don't tell what we are doing, we will treat you kindly and faithfully when the Lord gives us the land.

Narrator: Rahab let the spies down by a rope through the window. (RAHAB PRETENDS TO LET SPIES OUT WINDOW.)

Rahab: (WHISPERS) Go to the hills so the pursuers will not find you. Hide yourselves there three days until they return, and then go on your way.

34

Spies:	This oath you made us swear will not be binding on us unless, when we enter the land, you have tied this scarlet cord in the window through which you let us down, and unless you have brought your father and mother, your brothers and all your family into your house. If anyone goes outside your house into the street, his blood will be on his own head; we will not be responsible. As for anyone who is in the house with you, his blood will be on our head if a hand is laid on his. But if you tell what we are doing, we will be released from the oath you made us swear.
Rahab:	Agreed. Let it be as you say.
Narrator:	So she sent them away and departed. And she tied the scarlet cord in the window. (RAHAB TIES A SCARLET THREAD TO THE WINDOW.)

After doing this skit, go around the room and have each woman share one thing about Rahab's faith (such as an evidence of it or one way it impacted her, her guests, or her family), giving her the freedom to say, "Pass."

Have each woman share her memory work and any thoughts she has about it.

SCRIPTURE STUDY

DAY 1

The Dance Begins When He Takes Your Hand

Many commentators see the scarlet cord which Rahab put outside her window as a beautiful symbol of salvation. It is reminiscent of the scarlet blood of the Passover lamb which the Israelites were instructed to apply, as a sign, to their doors, so that the angel of death would pass over their homes (Exod.12:21–23). Jesus is called our Passover Lamb. We must put our trust in the scarlet blood He shed at the cross in order to be spared from the coming wrath of God. Romans 3:25a in the *New Living Translation* says: *"For God sent Jesus to take the punishment for our sins and to satisfy God's anger against us. We are made right with God when we believe that Jesus shed his blood, sacrificing his life for us."* When we trust in God's provision, we are "made clean in His sight" or justified.

If you have not taken His hand in salvation and you sense He is offering it to you now, how thankful you can be! The dance is about to begin!

Memory Verses

Begin memorizing Romans 10:9–10. Review this each day and meditate on it:
> *That if you confess with your mouth, "Jesus is Lord," and believe in your heart that God raised him from the dead, you will be saved. For it is with your heart that you believe and are justified, and it is with your mouth that you confess and are saved* (Rom. 10:9–10).

You may find it helpful to write this passage on a card and put it someplace you spend a lot of time (your car, bathroom mirror, kitchen sink) for review and meditation.

Read Romans 5:6–10.

1. What did Jesus do to pay for our sin?

2. Meditate on the memory passage to determine what God is saying through the following:

   A. What does it mean if a person "confesses with his mouth 'Jesus is Lord' "?

   B. Why is it important to "believe in your heart that God raised Him from the dead"?

   C. From whom and what are we "saved"?

   D. What does it mean to be "justified"?

Read Joshua 2:17–21.

3. What action did the men demand of Rahab to make their oath binding?

What symbolism do you see in this?

4. Is a person saved if he/she knows about Christ's death on the cross but doesn't personally put his/her trust in that provision? Why or why not? (Draw a parallel with Rahab's story.)

5. How did you come to understand the plan of salvation, of the need to respond personally to Christ's death and resurrection?

6. How do you see a person's perspective toward hospitality changed by becoming a Christian? (2 Corinthians 5:11–19 may be helpful to you.)

DAY 2

Following His Lead

How the Lord longs for you to allow Him to take you in His arms and follow His lead. In order to do this, you must trust Him. The reason we want to take the lead ourselves is due to pride (we think we can lead better than He does) and doubt (He won't really lead us).

7. According to Joshua 2:8-11, explain why Rahab was willing to follow the Lord's lead. List everything she had learned about Him.

8. What are some things you know to be true of the Lord that might help you trust Him to lead you?

Read Acts 8:26-40

9. A. What did the angel of the Lord tell Phillip? (v. 26)

B. What evidence can you find in verse 27–28 that the Ethiopian eunuch had a heart tender toward God?

C. In verse 29, who led Philip? What were His instructions?

If we are sensitive to the Spirit, He may show us who is open—and simply tell us to go and stay near them, or go and invite them over. He may not tell us where the dance will lead us, but He simply asks us to start following Him.

D. What happened next? (vv. 30–35)

E. And what happened after that? (vv. 36–39)

F. Put yourself in Philip's place. How do you think he felt?

Continue memorizing Romans 10:9–10.

Action Assignment

Purchase the ingredients for a meal which can be put together quickly to have on hand for unexpected company. Or, make a casserole and freeze it. Have a brownie mix in the cupboard. You may or may not be inviting people over, but at least you will be ready.

Then, and everyone can do this, watch and see what needy (spiritually, emotionally, or physically) people God brings across your path. When that happens, if it seems appropriate, invite them over spontaneously. If not, at least be friendly, be engaging, and see what happens next. Paul Little, author of *How to Give Away Your Faith* (InterVarsity Press, 1988) said that he'd never known of anyone whom the Lord had used in personal evangelism who hadn't had "an attitude of expectancy." I believe God would have us cultivate this attitude of expectancy toward the people in our path, being ready to obey the Spirit's prompting however He leads.

DAY 3

Hearing the Music

When we first fall in love with Jesus, we hear the music. But so often, as time passes, we take Him for granted, get busy with so many things, and stop hearing the music. When that happens, we no longer recognize the people God has put in our path. And even if we are persuaded to invite them over (perhaps by a family member) we don't make them feel particularly welcome. We can become Marthas (so busy we forget our guest) or, even, the widow of Zarepath. Today we will study this historical incident.

Read 1 Kings 17:7–12.

10. A. What instructions did the Lord give Elijah and why? (vv. 7–9)

    B. What did Elijah say to her? (vv. 10–11)

    C. How did she respond to him? (v. 12)

    D. Have you ever been guilty of giving this kind of welcome? If so, what do you remember doing and why were you that way?

Read 1 Kings 17:13–16.

11. A. What does Elijah discern is her problem? (v. 13a)

    B. What does Elijah then tell her to do? (vv. 13–14)

    C. How does this calm her fears of Elijah, her small provisions, and her imminent death?

    D. What fears keep you from being hospitable?

What truths (what music) do you know from God's Word that could speak to your soul so those fears can be overcome?

Read 1 Kings 17:17-24.

12. A. What happened to the widow some time later? (v. 17) Imagine you are a widow with an only son. How would you feel?

    B. Why does the widow believe this happened? (v. 18)

When tragedy comes into our lives, it is a common response to assume it is because of sin (John 9:2–3). I can identify with the widow's pain. When my husband was struck with cancer in his prime, we both were very aware of sin in our lives—how often we had gone our own way. We also knew we deserved nothing, though we pled for mercy. When it was clear Steve was dying, we certainly knew we couldn't be angry. We were thankful for the years God had given us. We also knew, from the truth of Scripture, that though He allows tragedy into our lives, His plans for us are good, not evil, and that one day, all things will work together for the good to those who are called according to His purpose.

    C. What does Elijah do? (vv. 19—21) How does Elijah exhibit both compassion and faith? Be specific.

    D. How does the Lord respond to Elijah's cry? (vv. 22–23)

    E. What is the widow's response? (v. 24)

13. Has the Lord ever helped your faith grow as a result of practicing hospitality? If so, explain.

DAY 4

Falling in Love

Author Ken Gire, in *The Divine Embrace* (Tyndale House Publishers, 2004), says that if you fall in love with Jesus, your feet will follow. If you have ever watched couples dancing, you can tell who is in love and who is not. Some are dancing, but they are not intimate. They are going through the steps, but are not engaged. Others are gazing into one another's eyes, entranced, moving as one.

The real reason we fail to practice hospitality is because we have lost our first love. We can't hear the music, can't trust His hand to guide us, and can't be His love to others. When we look at the early church we see many examples of believers practicing hospitality. Why? They were filled with the excitement of that first love with Jesus that spilled out into others' lives.

14. In the following passages, describe what was happening, the spirit you see, and any impact on others.

    A. Acts 2:42–47

    B. Acts 3:1–10

    C. Acts 16:13–15

    D. Acts 16:22–34

Read Revelation 2:1–5.

15. A. Who is speaking and how is He described? (v. 1)

It is Jesus, and the seven stars are the seven angels of the seven churches (Rev. 1:20) and the seven lampstands are the churches themselves. Jesus was telling this church that He was walking right in their midst. He does the same with us. He longs for us to hear the music, to take His hand.

    B. How does He affirm the church at Ephesus? (vv. 2–3)

    C. What does He have against them? (v. 4)

D. What three things does He ask them to do? (v. 5)

E. If they refuse to obey, what warning does He give? (v. 5)

16. What are some signs of a person in love? How would you assess your love relationship with Jesus?

Pray through David's penitential psalm—Psalm 51. Confess your sins sincerely and ask God for the strength to truly turn from them. Ask Him, as David does in verse 12, to "restore the joy of your salvation."

DAY 5

The Joy of the Dance

Most commentators believe Rahab was a harlot, as the Greek word *porne* is based on the word *pernemi*, meaning "to sell." It is usually translated a female prostitute, though it can be translated innkeeper, and some commentators (Adam Clarke, Josephus) support that interpretation. If Rahab was a prostitute, it profoundly demonstrates God's grace in her life. Not only were she and her family saved, she became the mother of Boaz. This line is mentioned in the genealogy of Christ.

> "By faith the prostitute Rahab, because she welcomed the spies,
> was not killed with those who were disobedient" (Heb. 11:31).

17. For what was Rahab honored in the Hebrews Hall of Fame? Looking again at the story in Joshua 2, explain how she demonstrated this characteristic. Consider the risks she took and what motivated her to take them.

Reread Joshua 2:12–19.

18. How was Rahab's family blessed by her hospitality? Have you seen the Lord bless your family through your hospitality? If you can share a specific example, do so.

19. According to Matthew 1:5, who was Rahab's son?

20. What practices of hospitality do you think you are passing on to the next generation?

ACTION ASSIGNMENT

What did you do?

Secret Sisters

Pass a basket and have each woman who wishes to participate put her name in the basket. Pray that God will guide as you pass the basket again to draw out the name of your secret sister. You should pray for this woman faithfully for the rest of the study. You can also send her secret notes and small secret gifts, such as muffins or flowers from your garden. The last week of this study the secret sisters will be revealed.

PRAYER TIME

If time is short, pray in a circle, each woman praying for the woman on her right, asking the Lord to strengthen her faith so that she can be obedient in hospitality.

If time permits, take prayer requests and pray in a circle or have "popcorn prayer." Popcorn prayer is prayer in which the leader lifts a participant's name to the Lord. Then whoever feels led prays a short sentence (just a "pop") about that woman. There may be many pops, or just one. When the popping stops, the leader lifts another name—and so on. For example:

Leader: Father, we lift Maurita to You.

Anne: Lord, please show Maurita and her husband if they should open up their home to their unwed pregnant relative.

Lori: Please give Maurita and her husband wisdom.

Cindy: I agree, Lord.

[silence]

Leader: Father, we lift Anne to You.

Continue with others.

Prayers & Praises

_____

_____

_____

_____

_____

_____

_____

_____

_____

_____

_____

_____

_____

_____

Four
Hospitality Begins at Home

W hile we are definitely called to minister to those in need in our world, we must not neglect our own families. It's a scriptural principle that if you cannot practice God's plan in your own home, then you may not have the ability to practice it beyond your borders (1 Tim. 3:4–5). This lesson will concentrate on learning to restore and encourage the members of your own household and extended family.

WARMUP
Call out some ways a woman might make a simple meal beautiful through the planning of conversation, atmosphere, or affirmation.

SCRIPTURE STUDY

DAY 1

Better a Dinner of Herbs Where Love Is

The book of Proverbs has much to say about atmosphere in a home. Often we can get so busy about the material that we forget the more important things. A good mother *does* make sure that her children are fed and clothed, but a better mother, while not neglecting the material, realizes how much more important is the nurturing of the soul through love, peace, and edifying words. Who has not had the experience of spending two hours making a beautiful meal only to have it ruined in fifteen seconds by a cross word? If you are single, apply this to your closest friends, who, for a single woman, often become her family. Today we'll study five proverbs about atmosphere. They confirm, as we have already seen, that true hospitality is not so much about the food, but about the heart.

At the end of the day, choose one of these proverbs to memorize.

Read Proverbs 15:16–17.

1. A. What does verse 16 teach?

   B. Do you know a family that exemplifies either the positive or negative of the above? Share something about it.

   C. What does verse 17 teach?

   D. Have you experienced both sides of the above? Share something about it.

Read the following translations or paraphrases of Proverbs 15:17.

Better is a dinner of herbs where love is,
than a fatted calf with hatred.

(NKJV)

A bowl of soup with someone you love is better
than steak with someone you hate.

(NLT)

Better a bread crust shared in love
than a slab of prime rib served in hate.

(MSG)

Do you have comments or insights on these? If so, what?

Read Proverbs 17:1.

2. A. What does this verse teach?

B. While similar to 15:17, there is a slightly different emphasis. What is it?

A meal of bread and water in contented peace is better than a banquet spiced with quarrels.
                                        Proverbs 17:1 (MSG)

C. Compare Proverbs 17:1 to 1 Timothy 6:6–8. How are these passages similar?

How can you learn contentment? How can you teach it to your family?

Discuss your family mealtimes. Do you make family meals a priority? Do you have any guidelines on how to make these times peaceful and loving?

3. What is the teaching of Proverbs 17:22?

4. What is the teaching of Proverbs 21:19?

Choose one of the following to memorize:

Better a meal of vegetables where there is love than a fattened calf with hatred (Prov. 15:17).

Better a dry crust with peace and quiet than a house full of feasting, with strife (Prov. 17:1).

A cheerful heart is good medicine, but a crushed spirit dries up the bones (Prov. 17:22).

> *Better to live in a desert than with a quarrelsome and ill-tempered wife* (Prov. 21:19).

> *Offer hospitality to one another without grumbling* (1 Peter 4:9).

5. What are you choosing and why?

DAY 2

How Good and Pleasant It Is for Brothers to Dwell Together in Unity

Psalm 133 is a psalm exalting the beauty of family harmony. It definitely is talking about blood family, but it is also a picture of the family of God. This is a psalm that was sung, and its poetry emphasizes gifts that "descend" from God. Three times the phrase "descending" or "coming down" appears, showing us that just as oil comes down from the prophet (who represents God) on the head of the priest, just as dew comes down from God to Mt. Hermon and then to the mountains of Zion, so does peace and harmony come down from God to families. When our families are harmonious, whether it is our immediate family or the family of God, it ripples out blessing to others. Guests who come into our homes are comforted, inspired, and strengthened to be harmonious in their own relationships.

Harmony is a gift from God. We should seek it with our whole hearts: in prayer, and in obediently living out the Scriptures which tell us the secrets of harmony. Harmony is "good and pleasant" to us, to others, and to God. It is what Jesus prayed for in His final prayer on earth: "that we may be one" (John 17:21).

Read Psalm 133.

6. A. What is good and pleasant? (v. 1)

   B. What do you think "live together in unity" means? Does it mean agreement on everything? If not, what does it mean?

C. What is the first "running down" comparison? What is the second "running down" comparison? (v. 2)

D. Describe the anointing oil according to Exodus 30:22–25.

E. According to Proverbs 27:9a, what do perfume and incense (or oil) do for the heart? How is this like family harmony to God?

F. What is the third "running down" or "descending" comparison? (Ps. 133:3a)

G. What do all three pictures (family harmony, anointing oil, dew) have in common?

H. What is the point? What is the application?

Read John 17:20–23.

7. A. Jesus has just finished praying for His disciples. Now, for whom does He pray? (v. 20)

B. What does He pray? (vv. 20–23)

C. Why does He pray this? (v. 23)

8. Share a time when you witnessed great harmony in a family. What did you see? Why do you think they were so loving and harmonious? How did it impact you?

9. How do you think you could be used of God to increase harmony in your:

Immediate family?

Family of God?

Keep learning your memory verse.

DAY 3

Iron Sharpening Iron

In *Traits of a Healthy Family* (Ballentine Books, 1984), Dolores Curran discovered that healthy families "are very protective of the time allotted to the family dinner hour and often become angry if they're asked to infringe upon it for work or pleasure. A good number of respondents indicated that adults in the healthiest families they know refuse dinner meetings as a matter of principle. They discourage their children from sports activities that presume upon the dinner hour as a condition for team participation. . . . And they never allow television to become part of the menu." Likewise, in many strong families, the conversation becomes as important as the meal. It doesn't "just happen," any more than a good meal "just happens." Here are a few ideas that have worked well for various Christian families:

■ A psalm or a proverb is read and commented upon.

■ A country is chosen and prayed for, or an e-mail from a missionary is read and prayed over.

■ A book of the Bible is read through systematically—a short passage followed by these questions:

What does it say?

What does it mean?

How could I apply this personally?

■ Everyone shares his high and his low from the day. The high is an opportunity to praise God, the low is an opportunity to talk about how to trust God.

■ A recent movie that has been viewed by the family is discussed:

What were the Christian values?

What were the non-Christian values?

■ A question is raised to be discussed. Use the front page of the newspaper, the questions people asked Jesus, or these standard questions:

Was there a way you spied God today? (An answer to prayer, an unexpected grace, a moment with nature, unusual timing, or a passage from Scripture that was especially meaningful.)

Was there a way you had to trust God today?

Was there a way someone showed you love today?

Did you laugh today? Why?

Action Assignment

Plan a minimum of two meals with "family" before the end of this week and also plan, knowing you must be flexible, some ways for the conversation to be sharpening. Be ready to report at the end of the week. Write down your plan here:

10. What word picture does Proverbs 27:17 give? What is the point?

11. Why were the Pharisees unable to sharpen and edify one another according to Matthew 12:32–35? What warning is there for us?

12. Write down your dream for making home a special place for your family. Be as specific as possible, going through the day, from the time they wake up to the time they go to bed. Keep a balance, in your description, between ministering to physical needs (fixing balanced meals), emotional needs (how you greet them), and spiritual needs (planned dinner conversations). If you are single, adapt this dream to ministering to your roommate, your extended family, or your closest friends.

DAY 4

Being Hospitable to Your Extended Family

I have a dear friend with three married daughters and a newly-married son. When the three daughters were critical of their new sister-in-law, their mother took them out to lunch to talk to them. She said:

> "We are family. You will lose your brother if you will not love his wife, for you will force him into choosing. He will choose his wife, as he should! You will also miss having a wonderful sister, for you don't even know what Josie would be like if she felt loved and accepted by you. Think about how she feels—she is the newcomer and she's intuitive—she knows you don't truly embrace her. . . .Love is a choice, and you have the resources in Christ to love Josie and make a difference in this family.
>
> I want you to love her, like you long to be loved, and the way Jesus has loved you. I want you to give her grace—the way you long for grace and the way Jesus has given you grace."

Today, two years later, they are all close. How good and how pleasant it is when brethren dwell together in unity!

Some of our relatives may indeed be difficult, yet as those who have been forgiven, received, and loved by Christ, we are to forgive, receive, and love those God places in our paths.

Read Numbers 12.
13. Describe the sin which Miriam and Aaron committed in this passage (vv. 1–2), how the Lord disciplined them (vv. 4–10), and how it was resolved (vv. 11–16).

14. What are some possible reasons that Miriam and Aaron had an inhospitable spirit to their new sister-in-law?

The text seems to reveal the reason was jealousy. It's possible prejudice was involved as well, for Zipporah, a Gentile born in Ethiopia, may have had a different skin color. Miriam was the one who was punished because the feminine form of *spoke* (v. 1) reveals her as the instigator.

15. Strained relationships between in-laws and other relatives often reveal the darkness within us. Has the Lord revealed to you any darkness in your soul concerning your relationship with your relatives as He did with Miriam and Aaron?

DAY 5

Amazing Grace

We truly cannot be loving in our own strength. Most of the family portraits we have in Scripture are full of rivalry and strife. Today we will look at a few positive family portraits. What makes them unusual and amazing is that one who was hurt offered grace. Phillip Yancey, in *What's So Amazing About Grace?* (Zondervan, 1997) says grace is amazing because it's not natural—it's supernatural.

The story of Joseph fills the last third of Genesis. Joseph was the favored son of Jacob. His brothers hated him, threw him in a pit, and then sold him into slavery. They told Jacob that his son had been torn apart by a wild animal. Years later Joseph is in a position of power and his brothers are in need. It would have been natural for Joseph to hurt as he had been hurt.

Read Genesis 50:15-21.

15. A. What did Joseph's brothers expect and why? (v. 15)

B. In what ways did Joseph's brothers humble themselves? (vv. 16–18)

C. How did Joseph respond to them?

D. What clues do you find for Joseph's ability to give his brothers grace?

E. What can you learn from the above that will help you give grace to people who have hurt you?

F. Is there someone in your family to whom the Lord is prompting you to show grace? Who?

G. What will you do?

Review Exodus 18.

16. A. How did Jethro, Moses' father-in-law demonstrate a hospitable spirit? (18:2, 5–6, 13–23) As a priest, he had additional authority to offer advice. What motivated his advice? (18:18)

B. How did Moses demonstrate hospitality toward Jethro? (18:7–12, 24–27)

C. What principle or principles do you see demonstrated in this story which may be applicable to you with your extended family?

Read Job 1:1–5.

17. A. How did Job's family demonstrate the healthy ability to rejoice in each other and celebrate who they were?

B. What principle or principles can you learn from this story which you could apply to your immediate and extended family?

Action Assignment

Have you done your Action Assignment? Share what you did.

PRAYER TIME

Ask each woman, in addition to any concern she has on her heart, to share one way God would have her be more hospitable to her own family. Pair the women according to how they are seated, and have them pray in twos. They should also pray for their prayer partners throughout the week.

Prayers & Praises

_____

_____

_____

_____

_____

_____

_____

_____

_____

_____

_____

_____

_____

Five
Home for the Holidays

At Thanksgiving, Christmas, and Easter our homes are filled with family, friends, and hopefully, those in need. God instructed His people in times of celebration to help them remember what He had done for them, and to rejoice in Him. When holidays have this focus, they become wonderful times of renewal. But this focus is often lost—and though the traditions may stay, the time is stressful and meaningless, even destructive to relationships. This session is designed to help you be a facilitator of God's grace during the holidays. If the holidays are far away, this lesson will be particularly valuable. Too often we try to find our way out of the forest when we are already in it. This study will help you make a map long before you enter the woods.

WARMUP

Share something about celebrations of holidays in your home growing up. Did this play any part in your coming to Christ? Why or why not?

Share your memory passage and any meditations on it.

SCRIPTURE STUDY

DAY 1

Against Forgetting

The days believers tend to commemorate are: the day Christ was born, the day He died, and the day He rose again. We also celebrate the time leading up to each, calling them Advent and Lent. While there are no commandments in the New Testament to celebrate these times, neither is there any prohibition against celebrating them. In fact, in the Old Testament, God sternly commanded His children to remember His acts, to not forget them, but to set up holy days to pass them on to their children.

Lauren Winner is a Messianic Jew who, in *girl meets GOD* (Algonquin Books, 2002), traces her journey to Christ. Before she realized who He was and that He was calling her, it was the Jewish holy days that helped her stay on the path where she could hear His voice. She was going through a dry spell and called her rabbi, telling him she didn't know why she was doing any of the rituals, and she didn't feel close to God. He replied:

> This is the beauty of Judaism. Even when you doubt, even when it doesn't feel like anything is happening, even when it seems like God is not around, you keep doing the mitzvoth. You keep saying the prayers…lighting the Sabbath candles, and making latkes at Hanukkah. The action will get you through the dry spells. Eventually the feeling that God is hovering in between your shoulder blades will come back (Lauren F. Winner, *girl meets GOD*, p. 60).

So Lauren kept praying, decorating the sukkah with fruit, and lighting the Sabbath candles. A week before classes started her senior year of college, she picked up *At Home in Mitford* by Jan Karon in a bookstore—a novel about a rector in a small Episcopal church. She read all the novels and reread them, thinking, *I want what they have.* Later, she writes, looking back on how God was wooing her:

> Sometimes, as in a great novel, you cannot see until you get to the end that God was leaving clues for you all along. Sometimes you wonder, "How did I miss it? Surely any idiot should have been able to see from the second chapter that it was Miss Scarlet in the conservatory with the rope (Lauren F. Winner, *girl meets God*, p. 57).

How like our personal God to communicate to Lauren in a language she, as a Jew, understood. While many Episcopalians have not held to the truth of Scripture, there are those who have. My first editor and gifted poet, Luci Shaw, said, "I love the way the Episcopalians show the truth as well as tell it." The high liturgical churches keep the church calendar, so it is not surprising that Lauren, who honored the Jewish holy days, entered into God's Kingdom through the Episcopalian door.

Certainly we know that many holy days are kept without heart, and God hates that, as we will see. But God loves it when we remember, when we keep the days with heart, and when we pass them on to our children. He loves it when we remember the poor and the needy during this time, whether they are poor materially or spiritually, whether they are in our own family, the family of God, or outside the family of God.

Read Psalm 78:1–11.

1. A. How does this psalm open? (vv. 1–4)

   B. What were the Jews called to do? (vv. 5–8)

   C. What happened? (vv. 9–11)

2. As you look back over your life, what were some of the clues that God was on a quest for your love?

3. Were any of these clues related to the celebration of holy days?

I grew up in a church that didn't hold to the Scriptures. Yet at Christmas and Easter the appropriate passages were read. We sang the Christmas carols and the hymns of the Resurrection. When I was confronted with the claims of Christ, I thought, "Do I believe what I heard and sang all during my childhood?" Also, Christmas was a huge celebration in our home—and though it was mostly about gifts and food—I had to think, "Why such a big deal?"

Memory Verse

Memorize the following:

> *Nehemiah said, "Go and enjoy choice food and sweet drinks, and send some to those who have nothing prepared. This day is sacred to our LORD. Do not grieve, for the joy of the LORD is your strength."*
>
> (Neh. 8:10)

While we live in the time of the New Covenant and are no longer commanded to celebrate the days from the Old Covenant, we can learn some important principles about why we celebrate, how, and what can be accomplished.

4. What is the command in Exodus 12:14? Why? (vv. 26–28)

Read Leviticus 23.

5. In each of the following, name the day or the feast and write a one sentence summary about it.

■ Leviticus 23:3

■ Leviticus 23:4–8

■ Leviticus 23:9–14

■ Leviticus 23:15–22

■ Leviticus 23:23–25

■ Leviticus 23:26–32

■ Leviticus 23:33–44

6. Do you see any pattern in the above that might show you some principles for the holidays?

Read Nehemiah 8.

7. A. Describe what happened and how it happened. (vv. 1–9)

    B. How did Nehemiah instruct the Jews to celebrate their revival? (vv. 10–12)

    C. What parallels do you see with the celebration of Christian holidays?

    D. What else characterized their celebration? (vv.17–9:3)

    E. What parallel do you see in how we should celebrate Christian holidays?

When Nehemiah restored the "Feast of Tabernacles," he intertwined the celebration of feasting and giving gifts with rejoicing in the Lord, reading Scripture, examining their lives, and the meaningful tradition of living in stick huts for seven days so they could imagine what it was like for their ancestors to be nomads for 40 years in the wilderness.

8. What do you see in the celebration of these holy days that might be applicable to us, who are under the New Covenant?

DAY 2

Celebrations Which the Lord Hates

The Lord often wept at how the Jews had perverted His holy days. They may have kept the outward ritual, but they lost the spirit.

Read Isaiah 1:11–20.

9. A. What question does the Lord ask in verse 11?

   B. How did God feel about the festivals the Israelites were celebrating? (v. 14)

   C. Why? (vv. 15–16)

   D. What did God long to see in their lives? (vv. 17–19)

Read Micah 6:1–8.

10. A. How does this chapter open? (vv. 1–2)

   B. What are some of the acts the Lord wishes His people would remember? (vv. 3–5)

   C. Describe the escalating offerings the Israelites offered in order to gain the Lord's favor. (vv. 6–7)

   Micah displays the absurdity of Israel's dependence on empty ritual and sacrifice to earn divine favor. Such reliance showed a profound misunderstanding of God's grace, for Israel's salvation was free and not earned. (vv. 4–5). Moreover, Israel's covenant

obligations entailed social justice and mercy, not mere liturgy
(R. C. Sproul, editor for *The Reformed Bible*, p. 1432).

D. What is pleasing to the Lord? (v. 8)

11. How might you apply the principles from today to your celebrations?

Keep memorizing the passage from Nehemiah.

Action Assignment

In Healing the Dysfunctional Church Family (Victor Books, 1992), David Mains writes: "Healthy families understand the importance of celebration." Plan a simple celebration for your family and do it! You don't need a birthday or Christmas! (Spread a tablecloth on the floor and have a midwinter picnic; put candles in a pie to celebrate a 100 on a spelling test; make Sunday special because it's Sunday …) What will you do?

DAY 3

Celebrations Which the Lord Loves

"Christmastime," Lauren Winner writes, "may be the hardest season for churches. We are inured not only to the Christmas story itself, but also to our pastors' annual rants against consumerism. Every creative attempt to make the season meaningful, to steal it back inside the church, away from the shopping malls and cheesy radio stations, has been tried, and most of those creative solutions have proved wanting. Perhaps that problem is that we don't know what the meaning of this holiday, of Jesus' pushing into the world, is. If we did, we wouldn't have to worry about consumerism; if we knew what the Incarnation meant, we'd be so preoccupied with awe that we wouldn't notice all the shopping" (Lauren Winner, *girl meets God*, p. 35).

Again, hospitality is about the heart. When our heart is in it, when we truly realize God's great love and are a vehicle for that love, we have celebrations the Lord loves. Our traditions are filled with meaning, our homes with guests in need of grace, and our hearts with love.

Read Exodus 12:1–28.

12. God had a purpose for each of the traditions that He instituted for the Passover celebration. Each of the following had spiritual significance for the Israelites, and for us as Christians. What was it?

A. A lamb without blemish

For the Israelites?

For Christians? (For help, see 1 Peter 1:18–19.)

B. The blood applied over the door frame

For the Israelites?

For Christians? (For help, see 1 Peter 1:19; Hebrews 9:13–15.)

C. Ridding their homes of yeast and eating only unleavened bread for seven days

For the Israelites?

The New Bible Commentary: Revised (Eerdmans, 1970) explains that no yeast was to be used because they would have had to wait for the bread to rise and the Lord's deliverance was going to be sudden. And the Feast of Unleavened Bread would help them remember "the decisive suddenness of the deliverance."

For Christians? (For help, see 1 Corinthians 5:1–8.)

The Wycliffe Bible Commentary (Moody Press, 1962) explains that yeast often symbolizes sin in the Scriptures. "And just as a crumb of leaven in the house of the Israelite meant judgment (cf. Ex. 12:15), so sin in the believer's life means judgment. Hence the need of discipline."

13. According to Exodus 12:26–27, what was the purpose for the traditions of the Passover?

14. If we follow this, our holiday celebrations should help us to remember, with joy, how God intervened on our behalf.

   A. When you think of the first Christmas, why do the events of that night cause you to rejoice in the Lord?

   B. When you think of the first Easter, why do the events of that day cause you to rejoice in the Lord?

15. Scripture, music, and many classic Christian books can enhance our joy at holidays, helping us to remember God's intervention. With this in mind, how might you help family, friends, and all you welcome to your home experience more of the joy of the Lord at:

■ Thanksgiving?

■ Advent and Christmas?

■ Lent and Easter?

DAY 4

Tradition!

Have you seen *Fiddler on the Roof*? Who cannot help but be inspired by the scene of the father dancing and singing with great heart, "Tradition!" Just as the traditions were meaningful in the time of the Old Covenant, so can ours be. Ours are not commanded by God, but many are inspired by His Words, His principles, and His love of tradition. Christians have instituted many traditions at Christmas and Easter which have been kept over the years. Originally, there was a purpose and a meaning for each of them, though many now keep the tradition without understanding the meaning. Let us restore the meaning!

16. Easter eggs, and possibly Christmas trees as well, have pagan roots. In any case, all of the following symbols can be used to represent truths from God. Would you be able to teach your children Christian symbolism of any of the following? (See Leader's Helps, page 118 after you give it a try!)

Candy canes	Easter baskets
Christmas lights	Easter eggs
Christmas trees	Fasting
Colors of Christmas	The 40 days of Lent
Colors of Easter	Holly and the ivy
Cornucopia	Wreaths

Many Christian families have instituted their own traditions, in an effort to help their children understand the meaning of the day. Here are a few ideas:

Halloween: This day desperately needs to be reformed, and churches in our community help by getting together to have a fair for the children. The children dress up as Bible characters, animals from Noah's Ark, or the prince and princesses they are in Christ. We have games and good food.

When visiting in Poland, I was moved by how they celebrate "All Hallow's Eve," a holy night of remembering believers who are now with the Lord. The families walk to the cemeteries carrying candles to place at their loved ones graves. Hymns are sung, and then they gather in homes to share memories and thanksgiving for their loved ones.

Thanksgiving: God instructed His people to remember the poor in the midst of their celebrations. Our family prays and asks God to reveal someone who is in need. Then, the weekend before Thanksgiving, we are "Thanksgiving Elves" and deliver a food basket, in secret.

Instead of a horn of plenty, we keep a basket on the table during the entire month of November in which family members put slips of paper when they think of one of God's blessings to them. These are read on Thanksgiving day and interspersed with our singing such hymns as: "We Gather Together," "Now Thank We All Our God," and "Count Your Many Blessings."

With each course at the Thanksgiving feast, we go around the table, answering one of the following questions: "What are you thankful for this year that you couldn't have been thankful for last year? What has God taught you this year that you are thankful to know? What three blessings are you most thankful for?"

Christmas: One evening early in December we unpack the manger scene. We read the Christmas story and as each figure is mentioned, we put it in place. Only Baby Jesus is left out—He isn't put in place until Christmas Eve. Meanwhile, our small children prepare the manger with sticks of hay. Each kind deed entitles them to place a stick of hay in the Savior's bed.

We bake cookies in the meaningful shapes of stars, sheep, camels, bells, and crosses and take them to our local prison. The warden lets us carol as we deliver our cookies.

Easter: Every Lent we give up all sweets to remember what Jesus gave up for us. On Good Friday, we fast the hours Jesus was on the cross (9 a.m. to 3 p.m.). I did this as a child as well, and it did cause me to reflect on Christ's sacrifice. I also remember how spiritually significant the baskets of bright jelly beans and chocolate eggs on Easter morning became. My mourning, like Christ's, turned to dancing!

Some of the traditions in our holidays actually have pagan roots. Easter is connected to mythology, and the goddess of spring. The bunny and the egg, for example, were symbols of fertility. Yet Christians have rescued and redeemed this celebration. Spring and its symbols can also represent the resurrection and new life—but instead of worshipping the goddess of fertility, we worship the One who was resurrected from the dead.

Likewise, the *date* of Christmas, December 25, actually has pagan roots. Two thousands years ago, pagans were worshipping a false god. For this reason some groups, including a few Christian denominations and also some cults, do not celebrate Christmas. However, again, just as our Lord would redeem and reform, turning ashes into beauty, so we should follow in His steps. Is it wrong to celebrate these days because of their pagan roots? Romans 14 addresses this issue clearly. In Paul's day, some believers wondered if it was acceptable to eat meat that had been associated with idols. Should they participate in something that had pagan roots? Paul made it clear that they were free to do so, but they were to celebrate the day as "unto the Lord." May we do the same.

17. Nothing that the Lord created is evil, but all has been corrupted to some degree by the sin of man. Yet the Lord *still* can rescue and redeem.

Summarize each of the following passages and look for a pattern.

A. Isaiah 61:1–3

B. Isaiah 65:17–19

C. Jeremiah 31:31–34

D. 2 Corinthians 5:17

18. What pattern do you see? How could this be applied to our holiday celebrations? To yours, personally?

19. Do you like any of the above traditions? Do you have any meaningful traditions you would like to share with your small group?

Read Esther 9:19–22.

20. What is the purpose of the celebration of Purim? What parallel do you see in the purpose of the celebration of Christmas or Easter?

21. How did Mordecai instruct the Jews to celebrate? Again, what parallels do you see?

22. The exhortation of the prophets, Nehemiah and Esther, is that the poor are to be remembered. Have you a tradition that helps you to do this at Thanksgiving, Christmas, and/or Easter? If so, what do you do? If not, what might you do?

Review your memory work.

DAY 5

Keeping a Balance

When we reflect on Christmases past, it's likely the most meaningful memories are those enveloped by love. Tom Hegg's bestseller, *A Cup of Christmas Tea* (Waldman House Press, 1982), tells of a reluctant visit to his great-aunt:

> *She stood there, pale and tiny,*
> *looking fragile as an egg . . .*
> *I forced myself from staring at the brace*
> *that held her leg.*
> *And though her thick bifocals*
> *seemed to crack and spread her eyes,*
> *Their milky and refracted depths*
> *lit up with young surprise* (p. 22).

As he looks around at a familiar home, decorated for Christmas and waiting for his visit ("Before my eyes and ears and nose was Christmas past . . . alive . . . intact"), as he eats the cookies baked for him ("impossibly good cookies she still somehow baked herself"), as he allows himself to be drawn out in conversation ("She was still passionately interested in everything I did") he says, "Like magic, I was six again, deep in a Christmas spell" and reflects:

> *But these rich, tactile memories*
> *became quite pale and thin*
> *When measured by the Christmas*
> *my Great Aunt kept deep within.*
> *Her body halved and nearly spent,*
> *but my Great Aunt was whole.*
> *I saw a Christmas miracle . . .*
> *the triumph of a soul* (p. 41).

Read 1 Corinthians 13:1–2.

23. A. What is the central teaching of these verses?

B. Describe a Christmas memory enveloped in love.

C. Take two of the following Christmas traditions and describe how you might envelop them in love: sending Christmas cards, choosing gifts, inviting guests over, baking, or ministering to the lonely or needy.

24. Sometimes preparations for holidays, particularly Christmas, make us anxious because, like Martha, we miss the most important thing, and instead, are worried and upset about many things.

    A. List your usual Christmas tasks and number them in order of importance.

    B. Is there any way to omit, simplify, or redeem any of the above? Write down your plan.

PRAYER TIME

Use the following names for Jesus as a means of praise: Immanuel (God with us), Good Shepherd (our Guide and Protector), The Alpha and The Omega (the Beginning and the End), Wonderful Counselor (Giver of wisdom), Mighty God (Omnipotent), Everlasting Father (Jesus, in the mystery of the Trinity, is one with God). Your small group leader should simply lift a name and then allow "popcorn p

raise." For example:

Leader: Immanuel

Margaret: I praise You that You are with us, Jesus.

Anne: And that You will never leave us or forsake us.

Jean: Yes, Lord.

Leader: Good Shepherd

Prayers & Praises

_____

_____

_____

_____

_____

_____

_____

_____

_____

_____

_____

_____

_____

_____

_____

_____

_____

Six

Hospitality to Those in Need

Jesus said, *"If you exchange greetings only with your own circle, are you doing anything exceptional? Even the pagans do that much"* (Matt. 5:47 PH). God commands that true believers extend hospitality to those who are in need. Romans 12:13 says: "When God's children are in need, be the one to help them out. And get into the habit of inviting guests home for dinner or, if they need lodging, for the night" (NLT).

These lessons are bound to be convicting to all of us. Remember that we simply cannot do these things in our own strength. But we can pray that God gives us the desire, energy, and will to obey, reaching out to those we would not, in our natural depravity, reach out to.

WARMUP

Read the following situations and have one or two women finish this sentence: Hospitality in this situation could make all the difference to me, if only. . .

Situation #1. Your husband is an unbeliever so you come to church alone. You sit down by yourself.

Situation #2. In order to learn Spanish, you plan to study at the University of

Seville. You are lonely and overwhelmed by the language, the bus system, and all the unfamiliar items in the grocery store.

Situation #3. You are a single parent, money and time are tight, and Christmas is coming.

Situation #4. You are 16 and you don't know the Lord. Your family is not Christian and you have been trying to fill the void in your life with sex.

Share your memory work and any meditations concerning it.

SCRIPTURE STUDY

DAY I

Although They Cannot Repay You, You Will Be Repaid

Hospitality seeks to minister, whereas entertaining is looking for some kind of reciprocation. The principle of not looking to man for our reward is throughout Scripture, but one that Luke particularly emphasizes. He tells us we must be different than the pagans who love just those who can love them back. Luke is not saying that we shouldn't show love or hospitality to our family and friends, for other Scriptures teach that we should. Instead, he is making a contrast to show how important it is that believers reach out to those who cannot reciprocate.

Read Luke 7:32–36.

1. List three groups of people to whom "pagans" are willing to "minister" and why.

Why must we be different?

Read Luke 14:12-14.

2. List four groups of people whom Jesus says "not to invite." Why?

Commentator Adam Clarke says: "Our Lord certainly does not mean that a man should not entertain at particular times, his friends. . . . What he condemns is those entertainments which are given to the rich, either to flatter them, or to procure a similar return." Clarke gives Job as an example. His home was open to friends and relatives, but history also tells us that he "had an open door on each of the four quarters of his house, that the poor, from whatever direction they might come, might find the door of hospitality open to receive them" (Adam Clarke, "Luke," *Clarke's Commentary,* Nashville, Abingdon, 1966).

Whom should we be sure to invite into our homes and why?

The maimed and blind represent a bigger category than just the literally maimed and blind—it represents those in need, those who cannot reciprocate. As you think about the people in your life, who might these be? Be specific.

Action Assignment

Invite someone who is in need (whom God brings to your attention) to supper—or make plans to visit the person. You will need to have extended your invitation or made your visit before you meet again with your small group.

Memory Verses

This week's passage and next week's passage are long, but important. An alternate option is to choose one and spend two weeks memorizing it.

> *Then Jesus said to his host, "When you give a luncheon or dinner, do not invite your friends, your brothers or relatives, or your rich neighbors; if you do, they may invite you back and so you will be repaid. But when you give a banquet, invite the poor, the crippled, the lame, the blind, and you will be blessed. Although they cannot repay you, you will be repaid at the resurrection of the righteous" (Luke 14:12–14).*

3. Meditate on Romans 12:13 and make five observations about this verse. What does the verb "practice" imply?

DAY 2

Humility and Hospitality

There is a link between true hospitality and humility.

■ True hospitality does not seek to impress, but to minister. Therefore true hospitality does not wait until one has a bigger or better home.

■ True hospitality does not look for repayment. Therefore, it does not hesitate to invite the poor, children, or our society's outcasts.

■ True hospitality is not embarrassed by guests of a lower social standing.

4. Between what two parables is the command of Luke 14:12–14 sandwiched? Do you see any significance in the context?

5. What Christian holidays do you tend to celebrate with "banquets" or "feasts" or "fancy dinners"? Have you ever included the people whom Jesus describes in Luke 14:13 in these occasions? Why or why not?

6. How might you better include those who are in need and cannot repay you at your Thanksgiving, Christmas, and Easter celebrations? (Consider international students, foster children, widows, the homeless, etc.) Be creative and specific in your brainstorming, drawing upon the passages in this session.

Continue your memory work.

DAY 3

True Spirituality

Just as the people in Isaiah's day had fallen into a pattern of redefining spirituality, confining it to certain practices, so have we. How we need our minds to be transformed through the Word. May the rain of God's Word fall on fallow hearts.

Review your memory verse.

Read Isaiah 58:1–5.

7. What spiritual disciplines were God's people exercising? (vv. 2–3) Why were they angry with God? (v. 3)

8. What did God tell them? (vv. 3–5)

Read Isaiah 58:6–7.

9. Meditate on Isaiah 58:6–7.

A. Describe what God longed to see in their lives.

The besetting sin of evangelicals is that we have redefined obedience in our own terms instead of God's terms. We've limited it to the things we are already doing, to "church things," rather than including all kinds of other things (Dr. Greg Scharf, professor at Trinity Evangelical Seminary).

B. Who are some of the people who come to mind in your life who are oppressed, carrying heavy burdens, hungry, or cast out?

C. In 7b, Isaiah tells us "not to turn away" from "our own flesh and blood." This is similar to 1 Timothy 5:8 where we are warned that if we do not provide for our own family, we are denying the faith and are worse than an unbeliever. Elsewhere Scripture makes it clear that each of us should carry our own load (a regular every day load) so this passage is not talking about enabling adult children or relatives with addictions. But there are relatives who are truly in need. Think about this particularly in regard to aging parents or grandparents. Imagine that one day you are unable to be mobile. What kind of treatment would you hope for from your children, or, if you are single, your extended family?

D. Is there an application to your life of verse 7b in regard to aging parents, aunts, grandparents? Others of "your own flesh and blood?" Be specific.

Read Isaiah 58:8–14.

10. What promises does God make in this passage? What conditions need to be met?

Whenever I read the high standards of God, I realize I must cry out for mercy, that He will put His desires, strength, and willing spirit in my heart. If you feel as I do, then ask Him for these things now.

DAY 4
• •

When You Do It to The Least of These, You Do It to Me

Hospitality has to do with the heart, and it may or may not involve inviting someone into your home. Remember that Jesus didn't have a home, but He was certainly hospitable.

Mike and Judy work together at the nursing home where my 93-year-old mother lived. Judy is a nurse, filled with the love of Christ. All through the day, she cheerfully meets needs, gives hugs, administers medicine and baths, and cares for residents. Her husband, Mike, works both as caregiver and janitor. His face truly shines with the radiance of Jesus. Once Mike told me he was inspired by a speaker at Promise Keepers who said, *Don't go for the gold—go for the golden rule.* "That's it!" Mike said, smiling. "That's what I want to do, every day." How we need more believers like Mike and Judy. When Mother Teresa visited wealthy America she called us poor. Amidst a list of sins, sounding like Isaiah 58, she pointed to the people in our nursing homes. "They are not visited, they look longingly toward the door—but you do not come!"

Often the things said when time is running out are the most important things. In His last parable, Jesus said that there will be a day when the sheep will be divided from the goats. It is so easy to talk the talk, but it is our walk that reveals if our hearts are truly with Him.

Read Matthew 25:31–46.

11. A. What is going to happen and when? (vv. 31–33)

B. What will He say to those on His right hand? (vv. 34–36)

C. What question is asked, and how is it answered? (vv. 37–40)

D. What will He say to those on His left hand? (vv. 41—43)

E. What question is asked, and how is it answered? (vv. 44—46)

While Scripture clearly teaches that salvation is based on the gift of God rather than our works (See Ephesians 2:8–9; 1 John 5:11–13; Romans 10:9–13) it also teaches that if a person has received Jesus Christ as his or her Savior and Lord, there's going to be a difference in his or her life. If there is no fruit, it may very well mean that we are not connected to the vine. (See James 1:14–19; John 15:5–8; and the above parable.)

How could you make it a part of your regular lifestyle to minister to the least of these?

DAY 5

Change My Heart, Oh God

When my husband and I were young, our pastor, Greg Scharf, preached on Isaiah 58. How convicted we were! I remember Greg saying that he and his wife were weak in showing hospitality to the needy, so often found it easier just to have someone in need move right in. Then they could be sure they were doing something! We took this to heart and began, on a regular basis, to invite people to live with us. Since then, we have had international students, missionaries on furlough, and daughters we adopted from orphanages in Korea and Thailand. Each has blessed us so. We have also sometimes invited people we should not have invited—but did so out of guilt. When we don't listen to the Lord, we can be working at cross-purposes with Him. Through the years, I have learned how very important it is to seek Him, and not just respond to anyone who wants to live with us because I want to assuage my guilt! There are those who think they are in need but actually could carry their own load—then there are others who are truly in need. There are also those to whom you are best equipped to minister, and those to whom you are not! Again, pray, be still, and listen! We need to continually realize our complete dependence on God—not only that He would put mercy in our hearts, but also wisdom in our heads.

Spend time in prayer. Ask the Lord to put His desires in your heart and His wisdom in your head. I have found it is often helpful to pray through Scripture. Pray through some of the passages you have studied this week.

Then, be still before Him. Write down anything He impresses on your heart, and any plan of action He gives you.

Action Assignment

Have you invited someone in need over or gone to visit someone in need? Report on what you did.

PRAYER TIME

Today, take prayer requests and then stand in a circle, holding hands. Each woman should say a sentence prayer for the request of the woman on her right. That prayer can be as simple as, "Lord, bless Nancy." If she feels she cannot say that, she should squeeze Nancy's hand and that will be a signal to Nancy to pray for the woman on her right.

Prayers & Praises

_____

_____

_____

_____

_____

_____

_____

_____

_____

_____

_____

_____

_____

_____

Seven
Unique Opportunities for Women

For most women, friendships with other women positively impact their emotional well-being. They enthusiastically describe the comfort, wisdom, and support that other women bring to their lives. It's natural for most of us to show hospitality to our close friends, and it's important that we do so, just as it's important that we show hospitality to our families. We can learn from Scripture how to make time with close friends constructive and meaningful.

Yet it's also vital that we stretch beyond our own circle of family and friends to "the stranger" and to "babes in Christ." Scripture has much to say about extending hospitality to these two groups. Women can make an enormous difference by extending hospitality to those who are new in town, new at church, or new in the faith. A direct command of Scripture is for the older women (we are all older than someone) to mentor younger women. Finally, women often have a natural doorway into the world of children, and can use their homes to make an eternal difference in children's lives.

WARMUP

Have everyone share either:

One thing she learned when she was a guest in the home of a godly woman.

———— OR ————

How we might do a better job of strengthening one another when we are together for coffee or lunch.

Share your memory passage and any meditations concerning it.

SCRIPTURE STUDY

DAY I

Train the Younger Women

I came into a relationship with Jesus after I was a mother, and my one-year-old was already out of control. I desperately needed mentoring. How thankful I am to women who invited me right into their homes so that I could watch them, and soak up how to be a good mother. I listened as Shirley told me she was training her children, that day, to close the door when they came in and out from the backyard. That was the boundary she had set, and she was training them to keep it, and training me to be a better mother. Each time they ran in or out, forgetting the door, she followed them, gently brought them back, had them close the door, and then praised them. *How much easier,* I thought, *it would be to simply close the door for them.* "Easier in the short term—much harder long term," Shirley said. "Correct your son, and he will give you rest," she quoted, "Yes, he will give delight to your soul" (Prov. 29:17 NKJV).

Memorize the following, perhaps dividing it into three days.

> *Likewise, teach the older women to be reverent in the way they live, not to be slanderers or addicted to much wine, but to teach what is good. Then they can train the younger women to love their husbands and children, to be self-controlled and pure, to be busy at home, to be kind, and to be subject to their husbands, so that no one will malign the word of God.* (Titus 2:3–5)

1. What are some of the descriptive phrases for a godly woman in the Titus passage? Explain what these phrases mean, using your own words.

2. What strikes you in this passage? Where does it touch your life experience? What is God saying to you?

3. Each of us should be mentoring and each of us should be mentored. What younger women are in your path to whom you could show yourself friendly? What older women could you approach who have gone where you are going, and have done it well?

DAY 2
. . . .

Edifying Fellowship Versus Idle Talk

Continue memorizing Titus 2:3–5.

Read Colossians 3:12–17.

4. On the basis of this passage, describe the kind of Christian fellowship which is edifying.

Read 1 Timothy 5:4–15.

5. Although these instructions were designed to help the early church decide which widows should be put on this list for support, we can glean some other applications from this passage. According to 1 Timothy 5, what do you learn about:
   A. The importance of showing hospitality to your own family? (vv. 4, 8)

   B. The importance of showing hospitality to others? (v. 10)

Reread 1 Timothy 5:13.

6. How are idle women described?

7. We are not as likely to go house to house gossiping, but we certainly can do it through the telephone, or even e-mail. Explain and evaluate your own practices.

Mary LaGrand Bouma writes in *The Creative Homemaker* (Bethany, 1973): "Kaffee-klatsches have become an object of scorn to many people who see them as a symbol of all that is inane and superficial in the life of a modern housewife. It is true that some women do sit together over endless cups of coffee, exchanging trivia. But a great deal of concern, wisdom, and love can be dispensed along with a cup of coffee. Important matters can be discussed over coffee in a woman's kitchen just as well as . . . in a pastor's study."

Action Assignment for right now!

Send an e-mail or note to a friend with the specific purpose of encouraging her. Affirm her strengths, tell her why she is important to you, share a way God has been ministering to you, and then write out a prayer for her, and pray it from your heart.

DAY 3

Hospitality to the Stranger

When my husband and I moved across the nation to Seattle, I was desperately lonely. I bravely went to a Bible study for young moms, and when the time came for prayer requests, all I could do was cry. What a scene I made! I was so embarrassed. Yet a couple of women responded with a heart for the stranger. They put their arms around me, prayed for me, and then invited me into their homes. They made all the difference in my life. Two of those women became lifelong friends.

Finish memorizing Titus 2:3–5.

Ruth was able to glean in the fields of Bethlehem when she and Naomi had just moved to town because God had commanded His people to be hospitable and generous to "the alien."

Read Deuteronomy 24:19–22.

8. What instructions does God give to His people? What reason does He give?

Read Exodus 23:9.

9. Have you ever moved? Do you know how it feels to be "an alien"? If so, describe your feelings.

Read Ruth 2:8–10.

10. What were some of the needs that Ruth had because she was new in town? How did Boaz meet them? Why do you think Ruth was surprised?

101 As Christians, we have a unique opportunity to stand apart and minister to "the alien." What are some of the spiritual, emotional, or physical needs that people have when they are new in town? How might you use hospitality to minister to them?

DAY 4

Hospitality to "Babes in Christ"

When I was a brand-new believer, several spiritually mature women invited me into their homes and mentored me through their examples and through their words.

> Anita invited our family for Sunday dinner. She lent me some Christian books and also gave me a radio schedule for the Christian station. She called me during the week to see if I'd started listening!

Lorinda showed me how to be a godly wife. My husband was gone all the time with a 90-hour-a-week internship, and I was angry he wasn't meeting my needs. Lorinda prayed with me, praying for Steve! God began to change my perspective, helping me to realize I wasn't the only one hurting in our marriage. He helped me to see this was a temporary time when my husband desperately needed my support, and I could make or break my marriage by my attitude.

LaVonne called and suggested we be accountability partners. We'd read three chapters of the Bible, record in a journal what God had impressed on our hearts, and then call the other to share what we'd learned.

Author Lucibel VanAtta quotes a pastor in *Women Encouraging Women* (Multnomah, 1988): "If every mature Christian woman took just one less mature Christian woman for about two years—parenting her, walking alongside her, seeing her do the same for others—exciting things would happen in the church."

Review Titus 2:3–5.

12. Imagine that you have a daughter, niece, or young friend in the church whom you think God might have you mentor. She is in your home for a short or extended visit. Considering the tide of the times she has to swim against, what are some practical assignments you might give her in order to "train" her to:

A. Love her husband

B. Love her children

C. Be self-controlled and pure

D. Be busy at home (The Greek word for this is derived from the word *guard*—a guard over the family and household affairs.)

E. Be kind

F. Be subject to her husband

Read Luke 1:6–7.

13. How is Elizabeth described in this passage?

It is noteworthy that Elizabeth was *blameless and barren.* Not only does this tell us that infertility may occur in women who are living righteously, but that Elizabeth had the faith to trust God in the midst of her denied dream.

Read Luke 1:34–40.

14. Why do you think Gabriel told Mary about Elizabeth? How did Mary respond? Why do you think she responded this way?

In my book *The Friendships of Women* (Victor, 1988), Win Couchman says:
   A mentor is someone further on down the road from you who is going where you want to go and who is willing to give you some light to help you get there.

15. How does Elizabeth fit Win Couchman's definition of a mentor? Using your imagination, what mentoring do you think might have occurred during Mary's three-month visit with Elizabeth?

I believe that, among other things, God wanted Mary to be with Elizabeth so that she could have experience with the preparation for the birth process—for He knew she would be giving birth on a bare barn floor. If we would be as sensitive to God's leading with older women as Mary was, we might be better prepared for the tough road ahead!

16. When you are in a difficult situation, to whom are you most likely to go first? (God? A peer? Your mother? Your husband? A godly older woman who has experienced a similar situation and handled it well?)

Read Luke 1:41–45.

17. Find at least five ways that Elizabeth encouraged this young girl.

Action Assignment #2

Choose one of the following and extend your invitation (or do it!) before you meet again with your small group:

A. Invite someone new in your town or church over for dessert or a meal.

B. Invite a less mature Christian over for coffee or lunch with the purpose of encouraging her.

C. Encourage a child, other than your own, spiritually.

DAY 5

Hospitality to Children

Howard Hendricks stresses concentrating on children and youth, for 19 out of 20 individuals come to Christ before the age of 25. Dr. Hendricks says: "We're really not too smart. We put 85% of our efforts where we will get 15% of the results—and we put 15% of our efforts where we will get 85% of the results" (Multnomah School of the Bible News, March/April, 1982).

When our five children were young, their friends were continually in our home, sharing meals, going with us to church, or Bible school, or camp. They took part in our family devotions while we acted out proverbs or read stories. We also had the great privilege of leading many to Christ. Their hearts were tender—it was like dropping seed in rich soil. How easily it sprouted! Today, how rewarding it is to see the ones who have become strong, green, thriving "trees." They are serving the Lord, and reproducing their own little sprouts.

18. What do you learn from the following passages about showing hospitality to children?

A. *"And whoever welcomes a little child like this in my name welcomes me"* (Matt. 18:5).

B. *"And if anyone gives even a cup of cold water to one of these little ones because he is My disciple, I tell you the truth, he will certainly not lose his reward"* (Matt. 10:42).

C. *"Train a child in the way he should go, and when he is old he will not turn from it"* (Prov. 22:6).

D. *"Better a poor but wise youth than an old but foolish king who no longer knows how to take warning"* (Eccl. 4:13).

E. *"Religion that God our Father accepts as pure and faultless is this: to look after orphans and widows in their distress and to keep oneself from being polluted by the world"* (Jas. 1:27).

19. How might you use hospitality to make an eternal difference in children's lives? What would work well for you?

Action Assignment

Report on what you did to make your time with a friend more meaningful.

PRAYER TIME

Pair off and pray together as friends. Have one woman share her concerns with the other and pray together, agreeing. Then have the other woman share her concerns and pray together. For example:

Sharon: Lord, please give Nellie wisdom concerning whether or not she should get a job.

Nellie: Yes, Lord—I agree.

Sharon: Please give her a peace about staying at home if that is Your will.

Nellie: Yes, Lord. And please help my husband and me to be like-minded.

Sharon: I agree, Lord.

Prayers & Praises

_____

_____

_____

_____

_____

_____

_____

_____

_____

_____

_____

_____

_____

_____

_____

Eight
Being a Good Guest

Just as a host can impart God's grace to his guests, so can a guest impart God's grace to his host. There's an art to being a good guest! Jesus knew it, and so did many who followed in His steps.

WARMUP

Have each group member describe a good guest. When should you bring a gift? When and how should you make your desires known about what you'd like to do? How do you write a meaningful thank-you note? What behavior seems rude? Thoughtful?

Share your memory passage and any meditations on it.

SCRIPTURE STUDY

DAY I
. . . .

Ministering as a Guest

This year, shortly before I began to update this guide on hospitality, I lost my precious fifty-nine-year-old husband to colon cancer. In June I went to the summer cabin I had always gone to with him. When I arrived, I was not only overwhelmed by loneliness, missing my life's companion, but I was overwhelmed by the jobs Steve had always so faithfully done: mowing the foot-high lawn, getting rid of hornet's nests or a dead mouse, carrying the kayaks to the beach or the picnic table from the garage...

Then four women friends arrived with a purpose in their hearts. For the next four days, they pitched in and helped me open the cabin, working into the afternoon. Then, each day, we'd stop and relax, sitting by the lake. They remembered things about Steve and freely talked about him, ministering to my soul. We cooked together, eating at the picnic table, watching the sunset over the lake. We sang hymns and prayed. We swam, kayaked, and played scrabble. Our laughter was like good medicine.

Then, after they left, they wrote me thank-you notes, telling me why they valued me as a friend, how they had been blessed by the time, and how they were praying for me.

There is an art to being a good guest. Again, hospitality is about the heart, about being a vehicle for God's grace. Guests are called to be hospitable as well as hosts.

Choose one of the following to memorize:

> *Share with God's people who are in need. Practice hospitality.*
> (Rom. 12:13)

> *Do nothing out of selfish ambition or vain conceit, but in humility consider others better than yourselves. Each of you should look not only to your own interests, but also to the interests of others.*
> (Phil. 2:3–4)

1. According to Philippians 2:3-4

   A. What should not motivate us?

   B. What should be our attitude?

   C. How could you apply this to being a good guest? Think of places you are invited and be specific.

2. What do the following proverbs teach? How could each be applied to being a good guest?

A. Proverbs 14:22

B. Proverbs 14:30

C. Proverbs 15:4

D. Proverbs 15:30

E. Proverbs 18:2

DAY 2

What Would Jesus Do?

Do you remember the initialed W.W.J.D. bracelets? Perhaps we should wear those when we are guests, for Jesus surely modeled being a good guest. W.W.J.D. doesn't always work because Jesus had the power and prerogative of God alone, so sometimes we cannot do what Jesus did. He could read minds and tell his host, Simon, where he erred in being a host. He could raise the dead and provide food for the multitudes. But His spirit, attitude, and caring questions provide a wonderful model for us. We should, indeed, ask, if not, "What would Jesus do," then, "How would Jesus have me respond?"

3. What does Jesus model or teach you about being a good guest in the following passages in Luke? (Be specific and creative!)

A. Luke 4:38–39

B. Luke 5:27–32 (Should we accept invitations to Christmas parties, reunions, etc., that will include mostly non-Christians?)

C. Luke 6:27–32 (You might apply this to being a guest in the home of a relative or business acquaintance who doesn't seem to love you.)

D. Luke 7:36–50 (How did Jesus express appreciation? How should you?)

The following thank-you note I received from a friend was particularly affirming, because, like Jesus, she was so specific:

> I looked forward to your invitation for lunch all week, and I was not disappointed! Candles at the table flickered your welcome, and your homemade cheese soup was creamy and comforting on a blustery day! But most of all I will remember your list of questions ("because you didn't want to forget anything"). How your interest in my life ministered to me! Thank you, Dee!

E. Luke 10:1–12

F. Luke 14:8–11

G. Luke 18:15–17 (How might you include the children of a host in your attentions?)

H. Luke 19:1–9 (Should we ever invite ourselves? Drop in on people? If so—why?)

I. Luke 24:13–32 (How might you come prepared to sharpen your friends spiritually?)

Action Assignment

Express appreciation to a host from your past. Write a note to the mother of a childhood friend who welcomed you into her home frequently! Or send an e-mail to someone who truly ministered to you through hospitality when you were new in town, new in the faith, or in need. Though you may have already thanked him or her, your note will be an encouragement to keep on practicing biblical hospitality.

DAY 3

Believers Who Model Being a Good Guest

Today we will look at believers in Scripture who modeled being a good guest. We will also consider being a "long-term" guest. I think it wise, if you are a host, to set up clear boundaries on expectations before a "long-term" guest moves in. When our daughter Sally recently went to live with a seminary professor and his family in Chicago, they helped her immensely by talking clearly to her about her "family" responsibilities. In addition to a small payment for room and board, she was to help fix supper, clean-up, and, once a week, clean the main floor and prepare dinner herself. It was wonderful to have such a clear understanding, and it helped her to be a good long-term guest. Long-term guests would be wise to think of themselves as family members who carry their load!

Read Genesis 39:1–23.

4. Describe how Joseph conducted himself when he lived in the house of Potiphar. Whom was Joseph trying to please?

5. Describe some ways guests can take advantage of their hosts. What should prevent them from doing so?

6. Mary stayed with Elizabeth for three months. What are some ways a long-term guest might minister to the needs of her host?

7. If you invite a long-term guest, why would it be wise to clearly articulate boundaries before a guest moves in? Give as many reasons as you can.

Read Acts 16:22–34.

8. What part had the jailer played in the suffering of Paul and Silas?

9. What changed the jailer's heart? How do you think he persuaded his wife to serve a meal at midnight to prisoners?

10. How did Paul and Silas minister to their hosts? What are some ways you might minister to your hosts?

Review your memory passage.

DAY 4

Receiving Hospitality Graciously and Wisely

Sometimes it is difficult to receive from others. In many cultures, it is a great offense if you will not receive graciously. Sometimes it is wiser *not* to receive hospitality, and the proverbs have specific warnings about that.

Read John 13:2–9.

11. Why do you think Peter was having difficulty receiving Christ's hospitality? Do you ever feel like this? Why?

12. Why is it important to learn to be served?

13. How might you personally apply the following Proverbs to being a wise or a thoughtful guest? (Take your time, meditating on each one.)

    A. *"Seldom set foot in your neighbor's house—too much of you, and he will hate you"* (Prov. 25:17). (How do you know when you are calling or visiting too often, or staying too long?)

    B. *"Honey seems tasteless to a person who is full, but even bitter food tastes sweet to the hungry"* (Prov. 27:7 NLT).

    C. *"Perfume and incense bring joy to the heart, and the pleasantness of one's friend springs from his earnest counsel"* (Prov. 27:9).

14. The writer of Proverbs also warns against accepting hospitality from some people. According to the following, what invitations should you decline and *why*? What would be contemporary applications?

A. Proverbs 7 describes the allure of an adulteress (you may wish to read the whole chapter) and ends with: *"Her house is a highway to the grave, leading down to the chambers of death"* (Proverbs 7:27). Likewise, Proverbs 9 closes with the woman Folly crying out: *" 'Stolen water is sweet; food eaten in secret is delicious!' But little do they know that the dead are there, that her guests are in the depths of the grave"* (Prov. 9:17–18).

B. *"When you sit to dine with a ruler, note well what is before you, and put a knife to your throat if you are given to gluttony. Do not crave his delicacies, for that food is deceptive"* (Prov. 23:1–3).

C. *"Do not eat the food of a stingy man, do not crave his delicacies; for he is the kind of man who is always thinking about the cost. 'Eat and drink,' he says to you, but his heart is not with you"* (Prov. 23:6–7).

15. What application might you make from the above proverbs?

Review your memory passage.

DAY 5

In Matthew 22:1–14, Jesus told a powerful story about a banquet God is going to hold in heaven one day. Throughout the ages, He has been inviting people to this banquet, through the prophets and through the disciples. Most refuse the invitation, but some receive it with joy.

Read Matthew 22:1–14.

16. Explain the main points Jesus was making through this story.

17. One inappropriately dressed guest angers God, and is cast out into the darkness. What clues do the following verses give us as to what this guest may have been lacking?

A. John 6:37

B. John 14:6

C. Revelation 19:7–8

Does the wedding garment represent salvation or a righteous life? John Calvin says this is a useless controversy, for you cannot have one without the other.

Action Assignment

Share what you think you will remember from this session about being a wise and good guest. Did you complete your Action Assignment? To whom did you write?

Review

18. Page through this guide, reviewing some of your Action Assignments, memory verses, and lessons. List three specific ways this is impacting your life.

PRAYER TIME

Take prayer requests, and then spend some time in popcorn prayer or praying in twos.

Prayers & Praises

_____

_____

_____

_____

_____

_____

_____

_____

_____

_____

_____

_____

_____

_____

Memory Verses

Week 2

The purposes of a man's heart are deep waters, but a man of understanding draws them out (Prov. 20:5).

Week 3

That if you confess with your mouth, "Jesus is Lord," and believe in your heart that God raised him from the dead, you will be saved. For it is with your heart that you believe and are justified, and it is with your mouth that you confess and are saved (Rom. 10:9–10).

Week 4

Choose one of the following to memorize:

Better a meal of vegetables where there is love than a fattened calf with hatred (Prov. 15:17).

Better a dry crust with peace and quiet than a house full of feasting with strife (Prov. 17:1).

A cheerful heart is good medicine, but a crushed spirit dries up the bones (Prov. 17:22).

Better to live in a desert than with a quarrelsome and ill-tempered wife (Prov. 21:19).

Offer hospitality to one another without grumbling (1 Peter 4:9).

Week 5

Nehemiah said, "Go and enjoy choice food and sweet drinks, and send some to those who have nothing prepared. This day is sacred to our LORD. Do not grieve, for the joy of the LORD is your strength" (Neh. 8:10).

Week 6

Then Jesus said to his host, "When you give a luncheon or dinner, do not invite your friends, your brother or relatives, or your rich neighbors; if you do, they may invite you back and so you will be repaid. But when you give a banquet, invite the poor, the crippled, the lame, the blind, and you will be blessed. Although they cannot repay you, you will be repaid at the resurrection of the righteous" (Luke 14:12–14).

Week 7

Likewise, teach the older women to be reverent in the way they live, not to be slanderers or addicted to much wine, but to teach what is good. Then they can train the younger women to love their husbands and children, to be self-controlled and pure, to be busy at home, to be kind, and to be subject to their husbands, so that no one will malign the word of God (Titus 2:3–5).

Week 8

Choose one of the following to memorize:

Share with God's people who are in need. Practice hospitality (Rom. 12:13).

Do nothing out of selfish ambition or vain conceit, but in humility consider others better than yourselves. Each of you should look not only to your own interests, but also to the interests of others (Phil. 2:3–4).

Leader's Helps

Your Role:
A Facilitator for the Holy Spirit and an Encourager

A Facilitator for the Holy Spirit

People remember best what they articulate themselves, so your role is to encourage discussion and keep it on track. Here are some things you can do to help:

1. Ask questions and allow silences until someone speaks up. If the silence seems interminable, rephrase the question, but don't answer it yourself!

2. Direct the group members to look in the Scripture for their answers. Ask: "Where in this passage can you find help for answering this question?"

3. Place chairs in as small a circle as possible. Space inhibits sharing.

4. Deal with the monopolizer:
   A. Pray not only for her control, but that you can help find ways to make her feel valued. Excessive talking often springs from deep emotional needs.

   B. Wait for her to take a breath and gently say: "Thanks, could we hear from someone else?"

   C. Go around the room with a question, giving people freedom to pass.

   D. Set down some ground rules at the beginning of the session. You can tell the group that you would like to hear from each person at least three times. So after they've spoken three times, they should give the shyer members time to gather the courage to speak up. When the problem is serious, pass out three pennies to each member one time, telling them, "Each time you speak, you spend a penny. When they are gone, give the others a chance to spend theirs."

E. So often in the Christian community we fail to speak the truth in love. Either we are silent, and let problems destroy, or if we do speak, it is not direct and loving. If this problem is not getting better, you have a responsibility to take the monopolizer aside and speak the truth in love. Here is what you might say: "You share easily, but some women are shy. They may have some wonderful things to say, but they need silences to gather the courage to speak up. I need your help." You could ask her for her ideas on how to help. She may surprise you! Some ideas are:

■ Star two or three questions and share only on those.

■ After she shares, she could say, "What does someone else think?"

■ She could watch the shy women's faces and if they seem like they have a thought, ask them if they do!

■ Count to ten before she shares to see if someone else will first.

5. The Action Assignments and memory work will be used mightily in your group members' lives. If they aren't doing these exercises, call a few from the group and ask them to be good examples with you. Soon the others will follow!

An Encourager

Most women who drop out of a group do so not because the study is too challenging, but because they don't feel valued. As a leader, these are some of the things you can do to help each woman feel valued:

1. Greet each woman warmly when she walks in the door. This meeting should be the high point of her week!

2. Affirm answers when you can genuinely do so: "Good insight! Great! Thank you!" And always affirm nonverbally with your eyes, a smile, a nod.

3. If a woman gives a wrong or off-the-wall answer, be careful not to crush her. You can still affirm her by saying: "That's interesting—What does someone else think?" If you feel her response must be corrected, someone in the group will probably do it. If they don't, space your correction so it doesn't immediately follow her response and is not obviously directed at her.

4. If this is an interdenominational group, set this ground rule: No one is to speak unfavorably of another denomination.

5. Plan an evening, lunch, or breakfast just to get to know each other. Play games, have a time of blessing each other, or just visit.

6. Send notes to absentees and postcards to the faithful in appreciation.

7. Don't skimp on the prayer time. Women's emotional and spiritual needs are met during the prayer time, so allot one third of your time for that.

Notes

_____

_____

_____

_____

_____

_____

_____

_____

_____

_____

_____

_____

_____

_____

Leader's Helps for Chapter 1

How Does Hospitality Differ from Entertaining?

Distribute the guides ahead of time and assign Chapter 1.

If you haven't distributed this study guide ahead of time, work through this first chapter together. After this, assign the chapter ahead of time.

If group members are struggling to respond to the last question in the Warmup, you might add:

A. What happens in a group where the attendance fluctuates so much that you have a different group each week? (It's hard to bond.)

B. What happens in a group where people don't do their homework? (It becomes a coffee klatsch.)

C. What happens in a group where everyone shares—the shy people as well? (It is richer.) How can we who are talkative help the shy people to share? (Hold back—ask what they think.)

SCRIPTURE STUDY

Reading the Scripture Aloud

Some people don't like to read aloud, but most don't mind. Say something like: Let's read Esther 1:1–9 aloud. Mary, we will start with you. Read a few verses and stop whenever you like. Then Susan, who is next, will do the same—and on around until we have read through verse 9. If anyone would rather not read today, simply say, 'Pass,' and the next person will continue.

Helps for Specific Questions

Question #4: Historical records show that this party was thrown shortly before Xerxes invaded Greece. He was inviting the Persian military leaders to his party, and he wanted to end his party with a bang. Vashti, in refusing to appear, may have not wanted to appear before what was most likely a drunken bachelor party. But her refusal embarrassed the man who was trying to display his power.

Question #13: He, Him

Question #19: Ask them to keep Xerxes and the Shunammite widow in mind to help them with their answers.

	ENTERTAINING	HOSPITALITY
MOTIVES	to impress	to serve
GUEST LIST	those who can repay you somehow	those whom the Lord leads you to serve
FOCUS	yourself and your impression: therefore food, home. . .	your guests and their needs
REWARDS	on earth	in heaven

Remind group members to start on their homework tomorrow with day 1!

Leader's Helps for Chapter 2

A Heart for Hospitality

SCRIPTURE STUDY

Helps for Specific Questions

Question #10B: As soon as the harvesters prayed a blessing on Boaz, he saw Ruth, his future wife!

Question #20A: Boaz provided for her safety (I've told the men not to touch you), for her food (help yourself), and for her not to be embarrassed. Note as well Ruth 2:15. A thoughtful host finds ways to protect a guest from having to ask where things are, or from a lack of privacy, or from a lack of a good pillow, a cup of coffee in the morning, and some basic toiletries such as toothpaste and soap.

PRAYER TIME

When praying for the woman on your right, it's best to pray clockwise. That way, you don't have to pray right after you have been prayed for, and may be feeling emotional.

Leader's Helps for Chapter 3

The Dance of Hospitality

WARMUP

Bring a few props for the Rahab skit to add to the fun. (A sheet for the flax which the spies hide under and a red belt, tie, or scarf for the scarlet thread or cord. Also, if possible, a few bathrobes for the Israelite spies, a scarf for Rahab, and police hats or badges for the Jericho police.) Position the players and take the role of the narrator. Don't worry about a great performance! Let it be rough so you don't take too much time from discussion. You'll have fun, and it will bring the story to life.

SCRIPTURE STUDY

Helps for Specific Questions

Question #2D: Just "just as if I'd never sinned."

Question #3: The scarlet cord is reminiscent of the blood that the Israelites used to mark their doors so the angel of death would Passover. Both are foreshadowings of the blood of the Lamb. When we trust in His blood, we too are saved.

Question #15d: Remember the height (what were you like when you first fell in love with Jesus) repent (do the U-turn) and do the things you did at first.

Question #19: Boaz.

PRAYER TIME

If "popcorn prayer" or "conversational prayer" is new to your group, you may want to demonstrate it first with two other prepared women.

Leader's Helps for Chapter 4

Hospitality Begins at Home

Helps for Specific Questions

Question #14: Verse 2 indicates clearly that jealousy was involved. If group members don't bring it up on their own, you might ask them why it's easy to feel jealous about a sibling or child whose priorities change when he or she marries. Also, why is this possessiveness displeasing to God? (We are supposed to "leave" our parents and "cleave" to our spouse.)

Question #16: There was a particularly good relationship between Moses and his father-in-law. Moses' openness with Jethro helped Jethro feel free to give advice. Though Jethro was the guest, he was eager to minister to Moses. And Moses, though he was a mighty man, was willing to listen to his elder. Both men seemed open to the Spirit of God.

Leader's Helps for Chapter 5

Home for the Holidays

SCRIPTURE STUDY

Helps for Specific Questions

Question #12A: A lamb without blemish.

For the Israelites: a perfect sacrifice.

For Christians: Jesus is the lamb, the perfect sacrifice.

Question #12B: The blood applied over the doorframe.

For the Israelites: By trusting in God's provision and applying it to their doors, they are protected, covered, from God's wrath. The angel of death would pass over them.

For Christians: By trusting in God's provision (Jesus' death on the Cross) and applying it to their hearts, they are protected, covered, from God's wrath. "Though their sins were as scarlet, they will be as white as snow," and they will be saved from hell.

Question #15: You might ask group members to name the titles of any favorite Thanksgiving or Easter hymns they sing in their homes. Also—the names of any meaningful books to read at holiday times.

Question #16:

> *Candy canes:* A shepherd's crook. Red: the blood of Christ; white: holiness.
>
> *Christmas lights and candles:* Reminds us of the light of the world. *"The people walking in darkness have seen a great light; on those living in the land of the shadow of death a light has dawned"* (Isa. 9:2).

Christmas trees: The evergreen reminds us of everlasting life, made possible by the gift of a Savior. Also, the Lord says of Himself, in Hosea 14:8: *"I am like a green pine tree; your fruitfulness comes from me."*

Colors of Christmas: Red: the blood of Christ; white: holiness; green: ever lasting life.

Colors of Easter: Purple: both repentance and King of kings; colors of spring flowers: new life in Christ.

Cornucopia: God's gracious provision.

Easter baskets: Mourning is turned to joy.

Easter eggs: New life.

Fasting: Fasting is done to receive wisdom, power, or to demonstrate sorrow for sin. It is also a time to learn that the Lord, and the Lord alone (not food, sex, television) can meet your needs. Too many people abstain from something but never run to the Lord—which is the whole point! Fasting must also be accompanied by obedience (Isaiah 58).

The 40 days of Lent: This tradition began in AD 313 when Constantine made Christianity legal and persecution stopped. Christians didn't have to be so committed and many felt a time of renewal to be wise. "Forty" was chosen because Jesus was prepared for His ministry with 40 days of fasting.

Holly and the ivy: The red berries, His blood; the pointy leaves, the crown of thorns our Savior wore.

Wreaths: The circle of eternity made possible by Christ.

Leader's Helps for Chapter 6

Hospitality to Those in Need

SCRIPTURE STUDY

Helps for Specific Questions

Question #3: If group members are having trouble coming up with five observations, help them by asking the following:

What are some of the key words? What do they mean?

Is this a question? A command? A suggestion? A promise?

What do you learn from the context?

What further insight does another translation give you?

What do you learn from cross references?

Question #4: Humility is emphasized in the Parable of the Ambitious Guest. The proud are not willing to have those whom society rejects in their homes. In the Parable of the Wedding Banquet, those whom society rejects were most open to the Gospel.

Question #7: Spiritual disciplines included: prayer and Scripture reading (v. 2); fasting (v. 3). The people were angry that God didn't seem to be noticing or answering their prayers (v. 3).

Question #8: God is displeased with religious activity that does not result in obedience.

Question #9B: "Loosing the chains of injustice" has many applications today. If group members are having trouble, you might ask: Who today, because of prejudice or a lack of justice, are deprived of life? Of food and shelter? Of loving parents? Of equal education or employment? Of hearing the Gospel? Of Bibles? Verse 7 has many applications to biblical hospitality.

Leader's Helps for Chapter 7

Unique Opportunities for Women

SCRIPTURE STUDY

Helps for Specific Questions

Question #17: If group members need help, direct them to find their answers in these verses:

> verse 42a—Elizabeth affirmed that Mary had been chosen by God for the highest possible honor.

> verse 42b—Though this baby could have been cause for shame in the eyes of the world, it was the highest possible honor to be carrying the Christ.

> verse 43—Elizabeth was much older than Mary—yet she bowed her knee to this young woman.

> verse 44—Even Elizabeth's baby, John the Baptist, recognized his Messiah—and Elizabeth told Mary so.

> verse 45—Elizabeth affirmed Mary's faith, saying, in effect: "Good for you—you believed God—and God is trustworthy!"

Leader's Helps for Chapter 8

Being a Good Guest

SCRIPTURE STUDY

Helps for Specific Questions

Question #3A: Being sensitive to your host's needs. I appreciate a long-term guest who pitches in without timidity or without being asked: fixing a casserole, vacuuming the house, taking the kids to the park.

Question #3B: Being willing to spend time with the unsaved. Definitely. See verse 31.

Question #4E: Being willing to let your hosts provide for you—especially when you are about the Lord's work. If someone seems very unresponsive to spiritual things, you might be wise to move on, spending time with more fertile ground.

Question #4F: There's a difference between allowing your host to provide the best for you and choosing the best. If your host is urging you to take the best chair or bed, then do—but don't seek it!

Notes

_____

_____

_____

_____

_____

_____

_____

_____

_____

_____

_____

_____

_____

_____

Notes

_____

_____

_____

_____

_____

_____

_____

_____

_____

_____

_____

_____

_____

_____

Notes

_____

_____

_____

_____

_____

_____

_____

_____

_____

_____

_____

_____

_____

_____

Notes

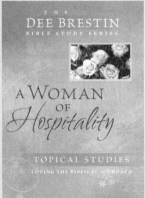
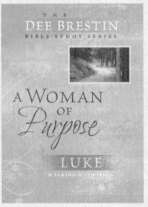
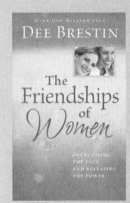

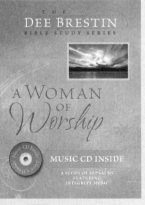

The Word at Work Around the World

A vital part of Cook Communications Ministries is our international outreach, Cook Communications Ministries International (CCMI). Your purchase of this book, and of other books and Christian-growth products from Cook, enables CCMI to provide Bibles and Christian literature to people in more than 150 languages in 65 countries.

Cook Communications Ministries is a not-for-profit, self-supporting organization. Revenues from sales of our books, Bible curricula, and other church and home products not only fund our U.S. ministry, but also fund our CCMI ministry around the world. One hundred percent of donations to CCMI go to our international literature programs.

CCMI reaches out internationally in three ways:

· Our premier International Christian Publishing Institute (ICPI) trains leaders from nationally led publishing houses around the world.

· We provide literature for pastors, evangelists, and Christian workers in their national language.

· We reach people at risk—refugees, AIDS victims, street children, and famine victims—with God's Word.

Word Power, God's Power

Faith Kidz, RiverOak, Honor, Life Journey, Victor, NexGen — every time you purchase a book produced by Cook Communications Ministries, you not only meet a vital personal need in your life or in the life of someone you love, but you're also a part of ministering to José in Colombia, Humberto in Chile, Gousa in India, or Lidiane in Brazil. You help make it possible for a pastor in China, a child in Peru, or a mother in West Africa to enjoy a life-changing book. And because you helped, children and adults around the world are learning God's Word and walking in his ways.

Thank you for your partnership in helping to disciple the world. May God bless you with the power of his Word in your life.

For more information about our international ministries, visit www.ccmi.org.